SAVAGE SEAS AND SFUMATO SKIES

SAVAGE SEAS AND SFUMATO SKIES

painting lyrical landscapes in brushstrokes and words

DEBRAH MARTIN

Published by IM Books

www.debrahmartin.co.uk

© Copyright Debrah Martin 2019

SAVAGE SEAS AND SFUMATO SKIES

ISBN 978-0-9933613-9-5

In memory of my lovely father, who painted in oils like an old master,
and who I wish I'd asked to teach me whilst he was alive.

Acknowledgement

With thanks to Tim Turan for allowing me to reproduce two of his beautiful photographs, Shotover Hill, looking South, and The Sky During RIDE's set @ Common People 2018. Please note that copyright for both images remains with Tim Turan. Tim can be contacted on tim@turanaudio.co.uk

I'm a romantic. I always will be, inspired by the juxtaposition of colour and form, life and art, people and emotions. It's why I write and it's why I paint. When I write I figure out things that I hadn't figured out before – about me and people and life in general. When I paint, I figure out there's nothing really to figure out at all because this beautiful world will do it all for me – if I allow it to. There's only one catalyst required; a cresting wave – a muse. This book is partly in recognition of MY muse – all the people in my life who've loved and encouraged me up till now – and it's also partly for anyone still seeking their own muse. May you find ways to express your own inspiration from the pages that follow.

PART 1: THE SEA

W hen I was little – like every child – I had BIG ideas about what I would do when I grew up and wasn't little anymore but BIG, and could do anything. Of course, when I grew up, I realised you could always do anything whether you were big or little, you just had to want to – and have the tools of whatever trade it was you wanted to master to hand to attempt it.

The sea has always fascinated me. I grew up by the sea and spent many a child-hood Sunday there, eating breakfast in our old green and white Hillman Minx car, parked up by the shoreline, when the sun was still low and the air still crisp, even in mid-summer.

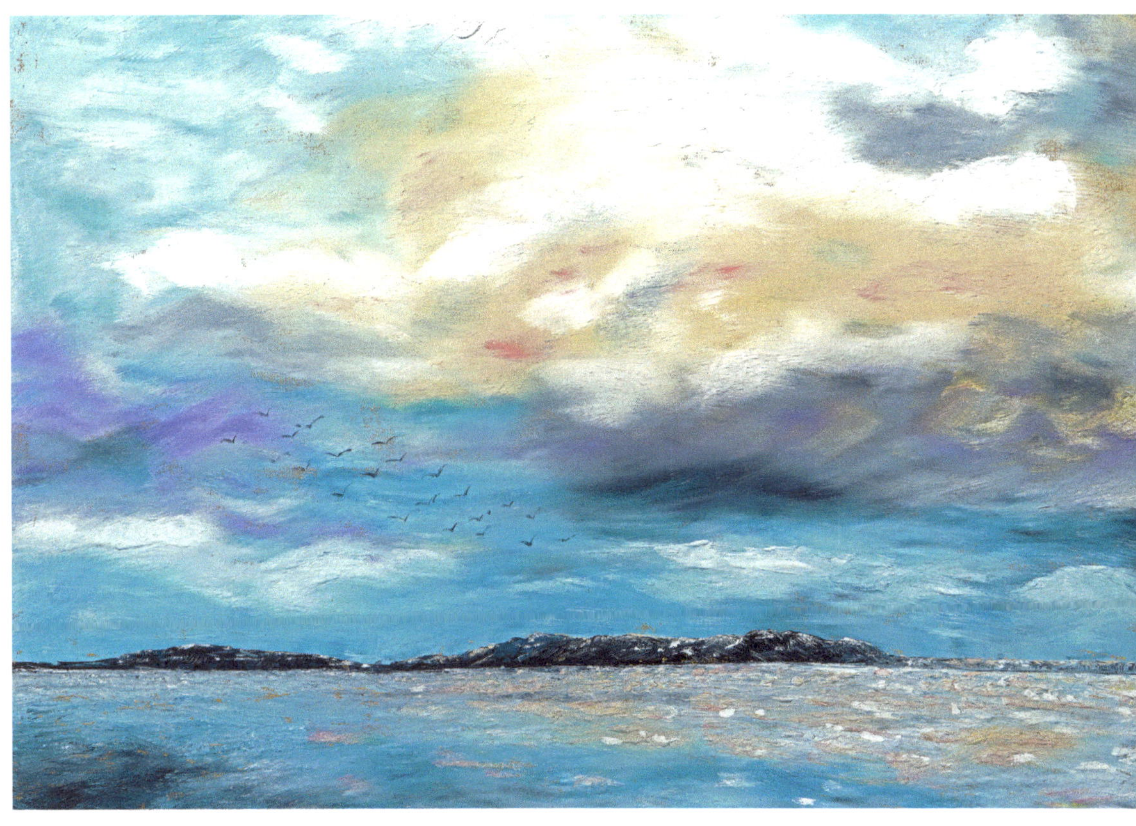

Once our cornflakes or whatever else we were required to eat before being allowed freedom to roam, had been forced down, my brother and I would scramble down the grassy bank and into the side of the Sandbanks pen-insula where all the small boats were moored. There, under the watchful eye of my father, who might be digging for bait or just wandering the shore, artist's eye alert for angles and lines and colour, we would wade out to the smallest dinghies and perch on their cramped decks, swinging our feet in the sea and scattering starfish with our toes.

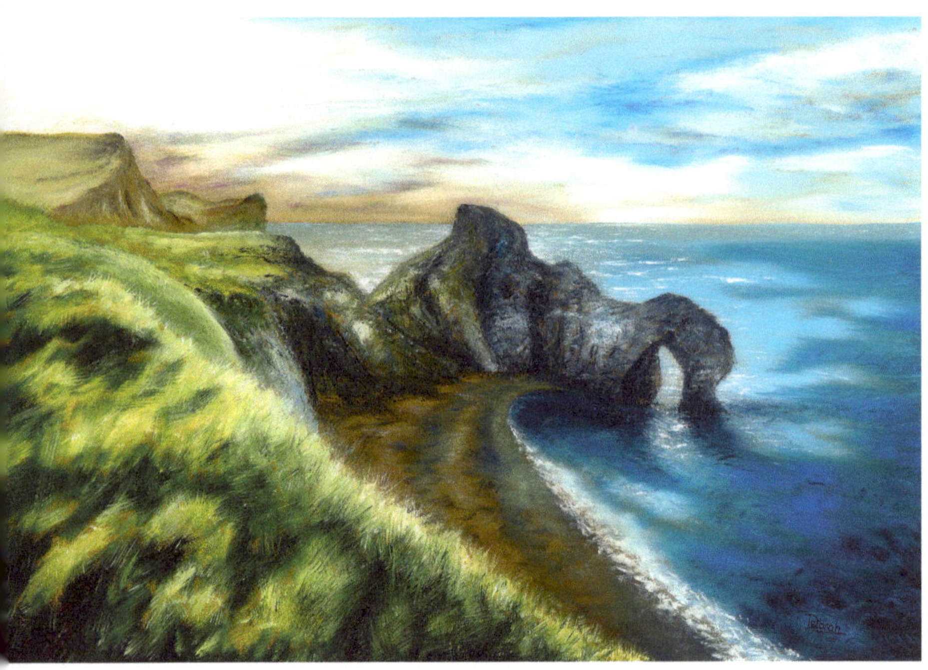

Or we would rove the shallows, catching tiny crabs in our buckets so we could set them free on the claggy sand by the grass bank, and cheer them on as they scuttled sideways back into the water. Sometimes we'd wallow in the shallows, bouncing and rolling like small hippos, covering ourselves in sticky brown sand and pretending we were mud bathing. Once, we filled my swimming costume until it ballooned with muddy sand, and my despairing father had to take me and my billowing, overstretched costume across the road to the longer golden strip that Sandbanks is renowned for and toss me about in the incoming wavelets until the sand bump was ejected, grain by grain, my brother and I laughing and laughing all the time.

They were happy days and I had a happy childhood, but I know the sea isn't always a friend. For me the sea is an ambiguity – always changing. Sometimes it is the stuff of happy childhood memories, simultaneously sweet and salty. Sometimes it is the stuff of nightmares, its overwhelming power swelling over the land in a tide of terror.

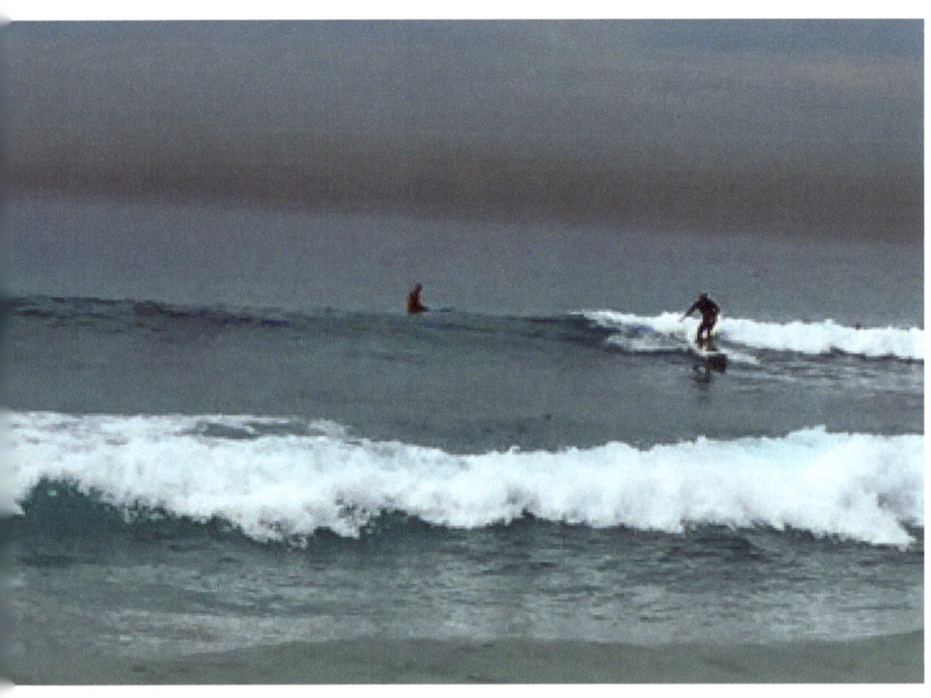

This is Bondi Beach, and yes, the sky really was that colour. When you look; really look around you and open your eyes to the possibility of seeing colours beyond the ones you anticipate seeing – brown for trees, blue for skies, green for grass – you suddenly see a world full of the most extraordinary blends of tone, palette and depth of hue. Blue is never just blue, green never just green, and brown? Well, you get the idea … We truly do live in an amazing world. We only need to open our eyes to see it.

Being so in love with the sea, of course I had to paint this scene, and as you will see a little further on, also take a little liberty with it. The other trick to seeing is seeing what could be there too. Does that make me a romanticist, a fantasist or an illusionist? I don't know. I do believe it makes me – and you – an artist, because we all see something profoundly unique to only us. Some scientists will have you consider the possibility that everything we see is unique only to us and the person standing only a fraction to your left or right sees something completely different to you, built from their own unique view of the world – created by the constant flux of molecules called neurotransmitters dancing their own particular dance through the brain. Every thought, dream or action is born of neurotransmitters, jumping and twisting their way from neuron to receptor. So much potential – and so much beauty and creativity – is stored in our complex and convoluted perception of the world. Let's release some of it here in colour and form…

This is Bondi Beach in the making – step 1: a scratch-card of line and shape.

You will notice the background I am painting onto is yellow – Yellow Ochre to be precise. This is my choice of under-painting, for two reasons:

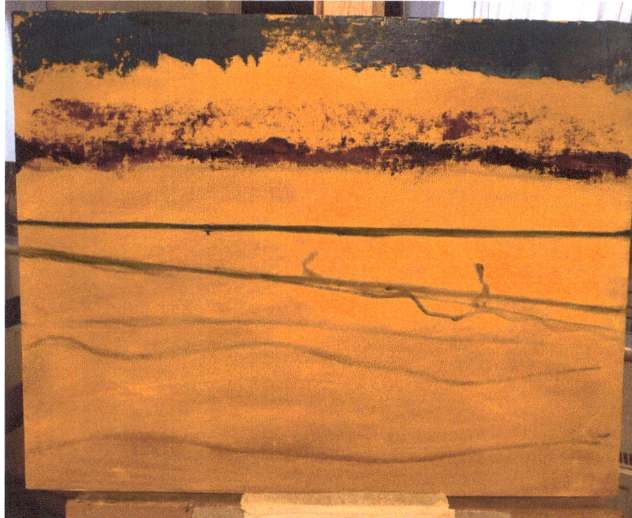

1. The colour is warm and I like a backlight of sunshine behind whatever I paint. I love sunshine and I love light and how it can transform the simplest scene. What better than an underlayer of sunshine to shine through to the top image?

2. I can see what I've painted and where – yes pragmatism comes into it too!

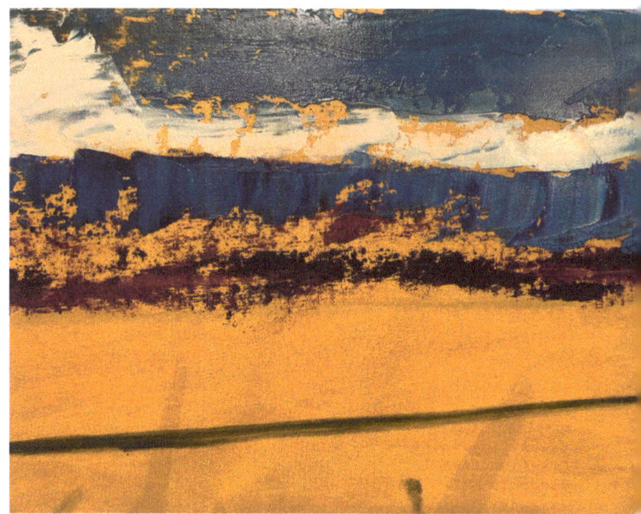

I have already started to fill in some of the base colours. The blue shade for the sky is made up of Cerulean Blue, French Ultramarine, Payne's Grey and Titanium White. It's a murky, foreboding sky with that gash of threatening red – or rather a mix of Permanent Rose and Permanent Mauve. Like I said before, blue is never just blue, green never just green, and so on. Be bold. I use a palette knife to block in colour. It's a speedy process and makes me less precious about getting things exact. Creativity and bravery go hand in hand.

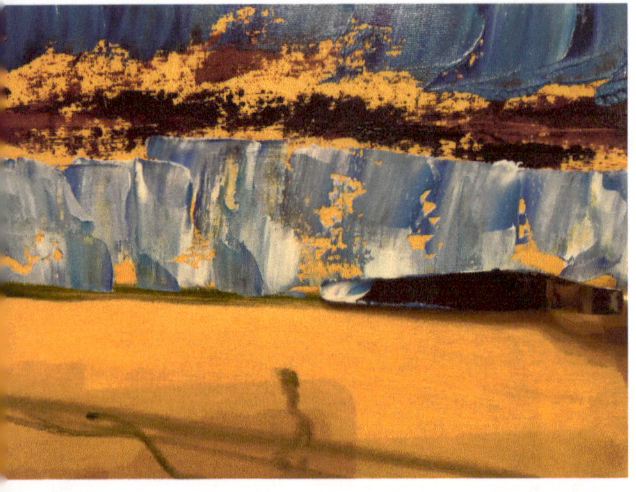

I block in all the main colours, including the highlights. Don't worry if it looks a mess at first. Building blocks are never pretty, but once pointed and tidied, they have a rare beauty of line and form.

Just watch what happens when you start to blend them.

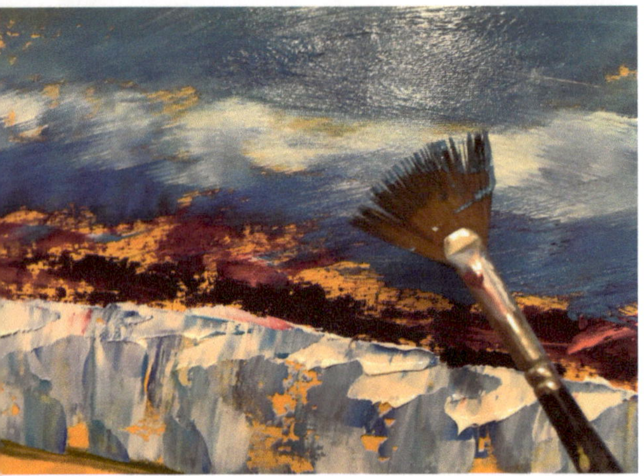

And then blend them again…

I am continually going back and adding more texture and more highlights and lowlights as I blend the colours.

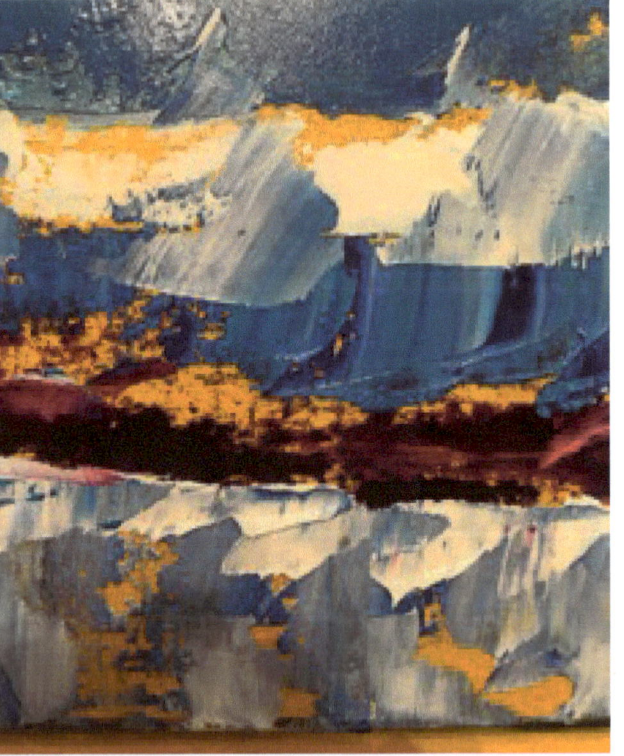

It may take several layers and several blendings to achieve a cohesive cloud and sky formation. Keep working on the layers, highlights and lowlights until they have flowed into each other in the same way that clouds and sky merge.

For this stage of the painting I have started with a Winsor and Newton 'Winton' fan brush and alternated it with a Pro Arte Series F Fan brush, number 50686513. I also use a Daler D55 'Dalon'.

Some of my brushes were inherited from my father so check around for suitable substitutes if the ones I refer to are unavailable. They are all moderately firm, but with good give, the Pro Arte, made of sable and the 'Winton' of hog hair. Later on, you will see I also use a very soft 'Silverline' number 10 brush from Jacksons – which has the most perfect smoothing effect on even the firmest of brushstrokes – and sometimes a tiny 1 cm fan brush, probably designed more for watercolour than oils, but it is perfect for the smallest spaces and the tiniest of details.

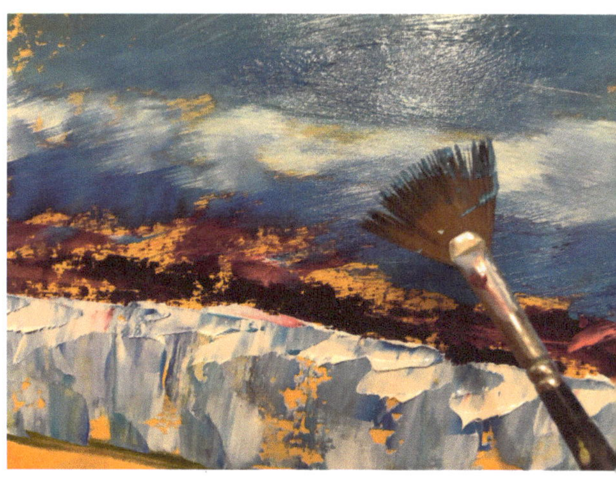

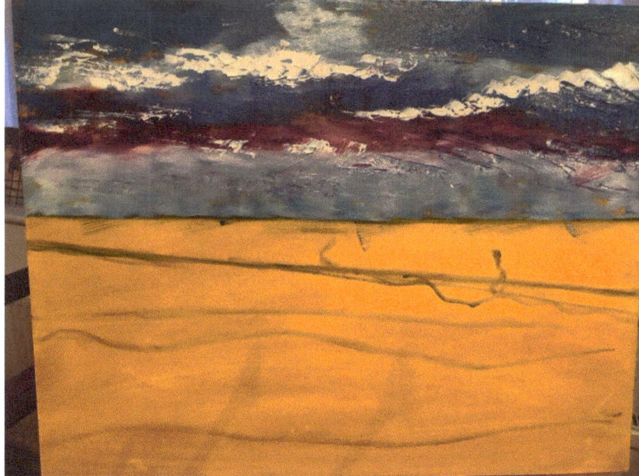

Change your brushes over regularly, cleaning them of residual paint and drying them fully, so they retain their softness and malleability and so there isn't too much colour contamination as you are completing the blending process.

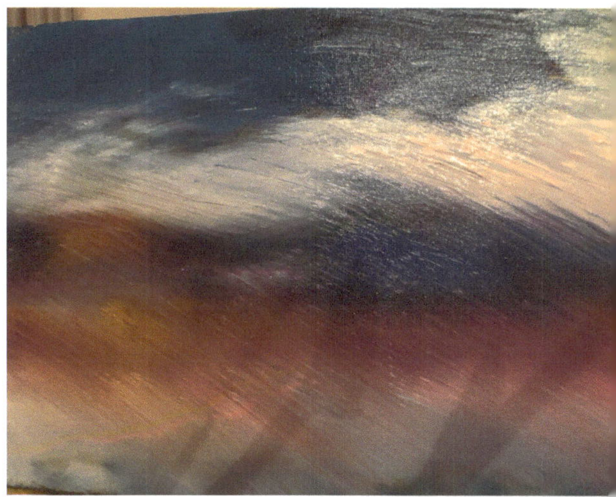

Once you are happy with the general shape, colour and texture of the sky, move onto the lower area of the painting – the sea.

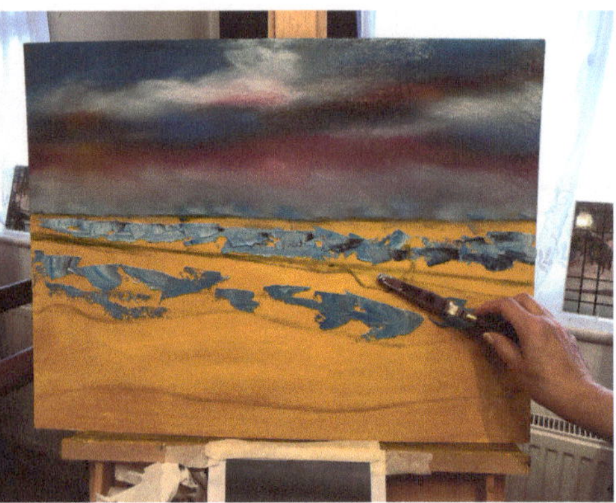 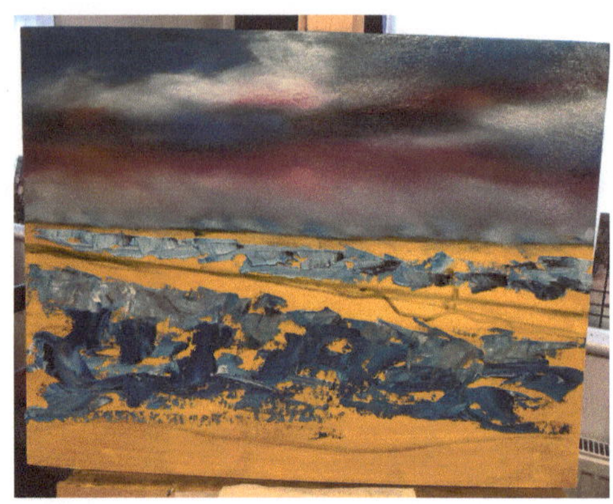 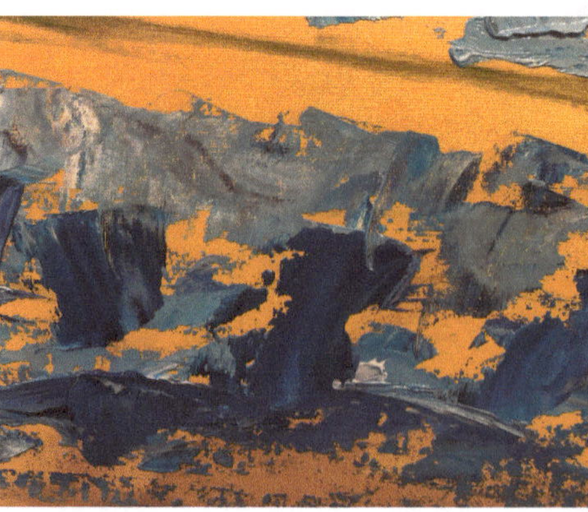

Start with blocking in the main contextual colour of the sea. In this case I have mirrored the Cerulean Blue, French Ultramarine, Payne's Grey and Titanium White of the sky because sea and sky bounce off each other and reflect each other's tones. However, I have also added in some Sap Green and Cadmium Yellow Deep to pick up the deeper undertow of the sea's depths and to add some distinction between sea and sky.

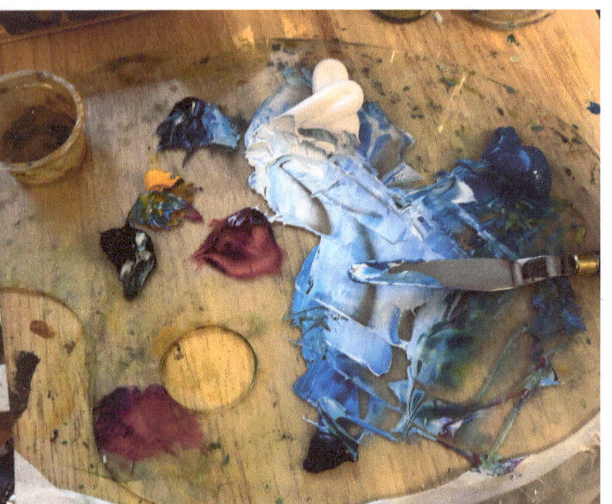

There is also a hint of Permanent Rose/Permanent Mauve in some of the darker undertones, which I will pick up on later.

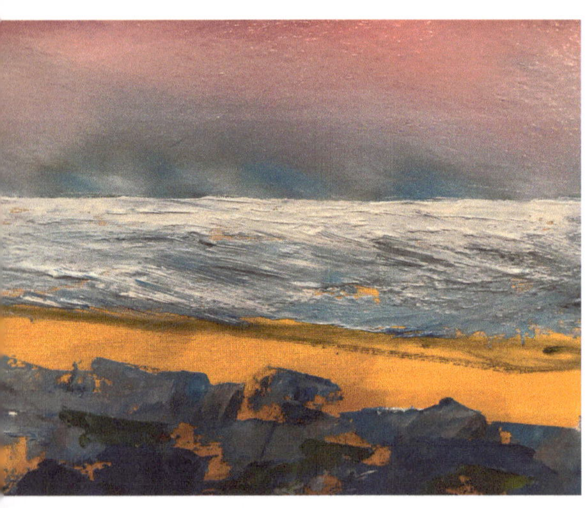

Now smooth the blocks of paint without losing their texture, and follow the line of a wave; the sea is fluid, the sky is diffuse. They are different movements and painting is also about movement and how that affects colour and form. Find the right movement and you will define the soul of whatever you are painting.

The horizon isn't so firmly defined in this image as it often is in images of the sea, so after delineating the two, I have deliberately blended sea and sky into each other using first the 'Winton' brush, followed by my tiny 1 cm fan brush.

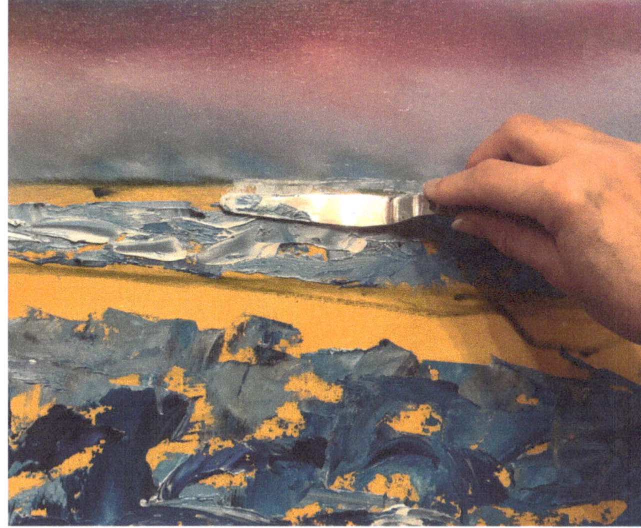

Continue to soften and form the surface of the higher area of the sea so it implies subtle movement, a swell building to a wave, but smooth, and untroubled – a place of safety for a surfer to hover, waiting to ride the next wave.

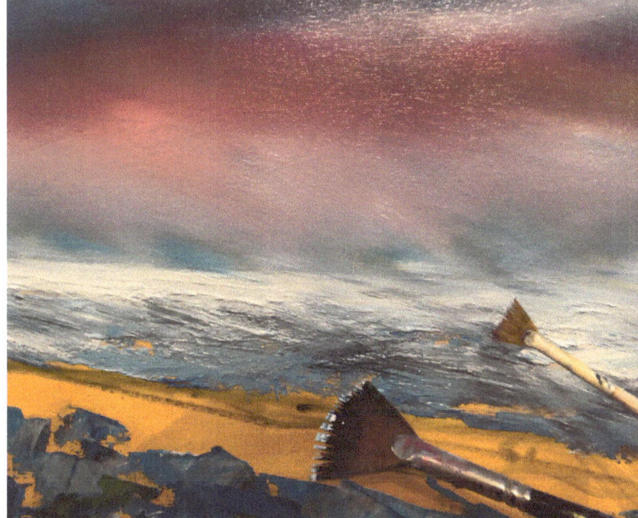

Under the higher area, a wave is beginning to crest ready to topple and crash into the shore. This is where the deepest undertow and darkest undertones are seen. This is also where sap green will enhance the darkest shade of sea blue, made up of Payne's Grey and French Ultramarine, but also Permanent Mauve and Permanent Rose that threaten from the evening sky.

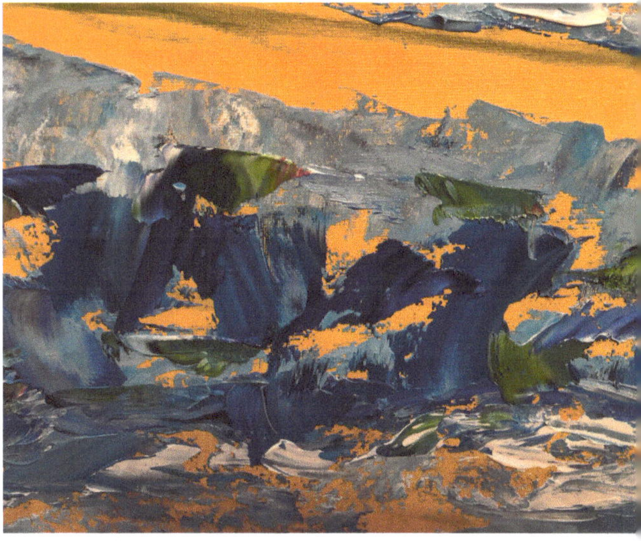

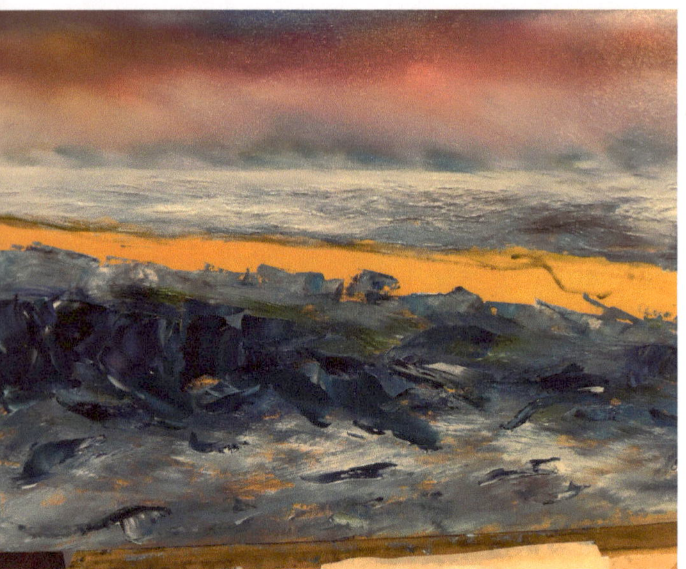

Soften, blend, and add highlights and lowlights as necessary to define the movement of the cresting wave – and stand back often to see how the wave movement is forming with your brushstrokes and blending…
(This is where the softest fan brush I have, my Silverline number 10 is perfect).

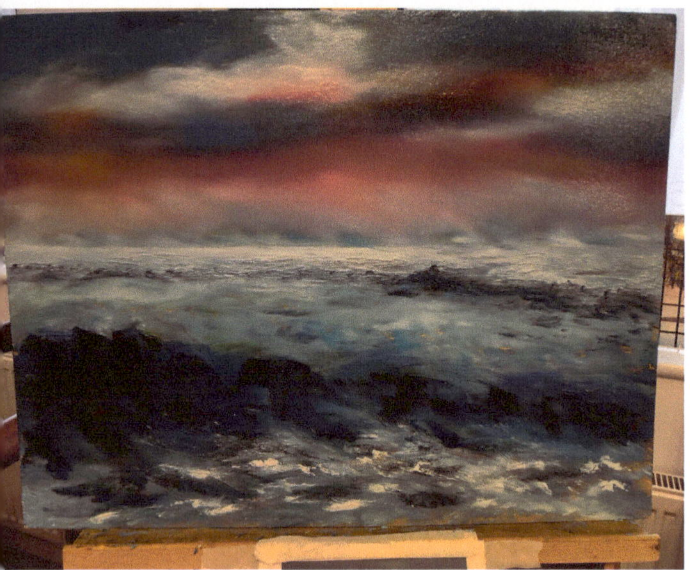

Finally, you have your sea in totality – only missing the crests of the waves and the surfers themselves.

Now you are itching to ride the wave yourself but be patient and leave it for a day or two for the sea base to harden off before painting in the crests so that the Titanium White foam isn't absorbed into the sea itself before it can spill over the canvas like a real wave.

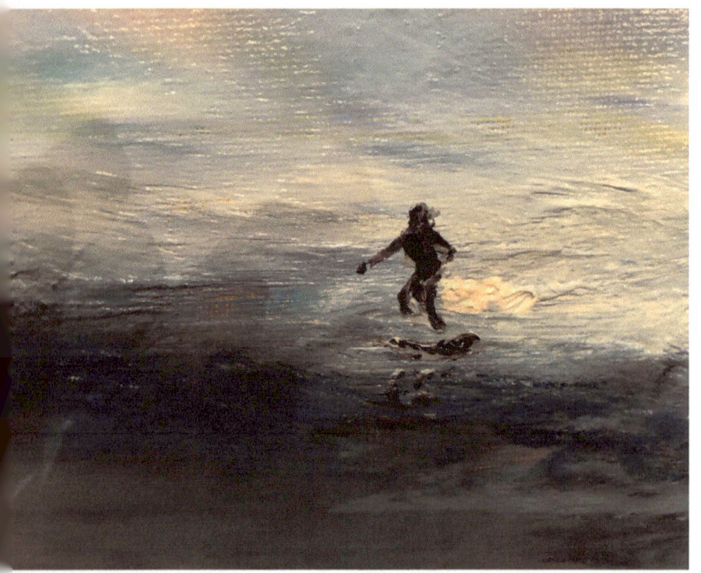

Start with the surfers …

Sketch in the surfers – they are forms only – using Liquin fine detail medium to thin paint so you can work in detail. Liquin thins paint so it is easier to use in tiny amounts.

Once the figures are sketched in, work around them, forming the distant wave and crest that they are riding. I used a combination of a small brush and a palette knife to give texture to the spume.

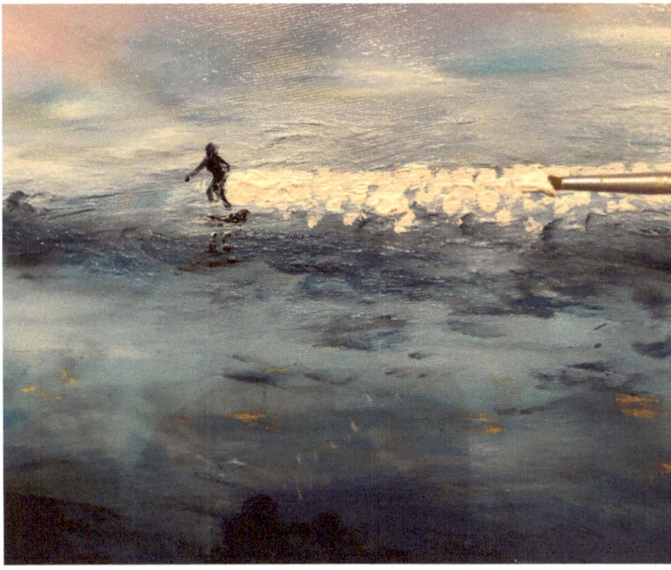

Remember to carry the spume from the wave crest down into its depths too.

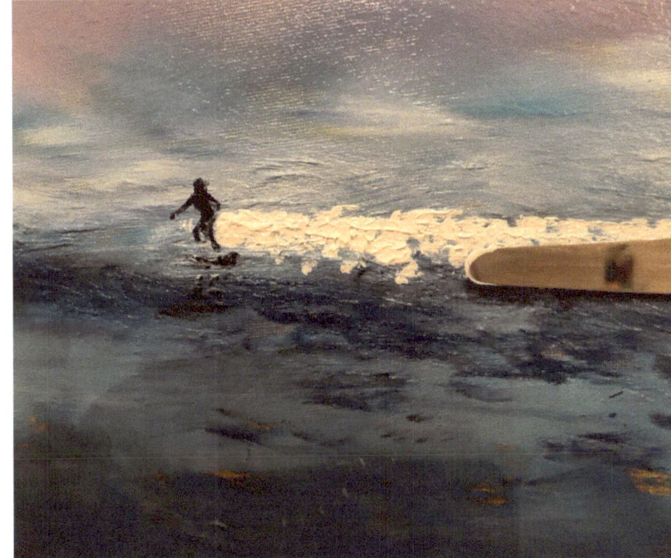

Then add in the undertones and darker edges that define the crest of the wave, but soften them with sweeping, upward strokes of the fan brush. I used my softest for this, the Silverline 10.

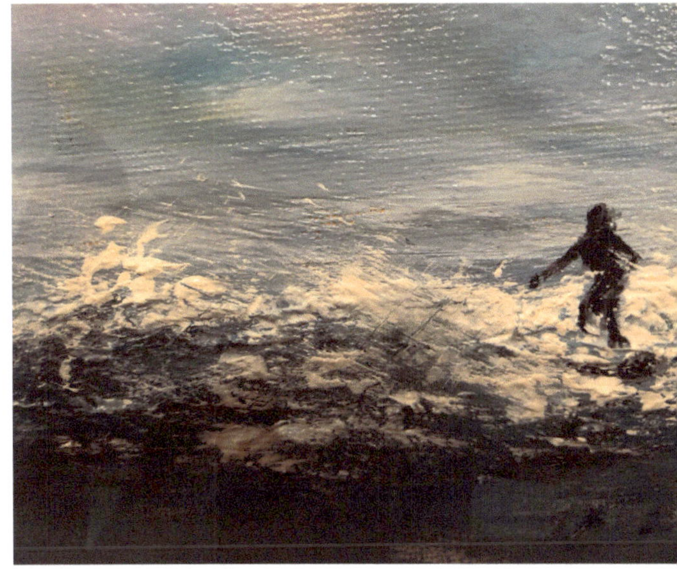

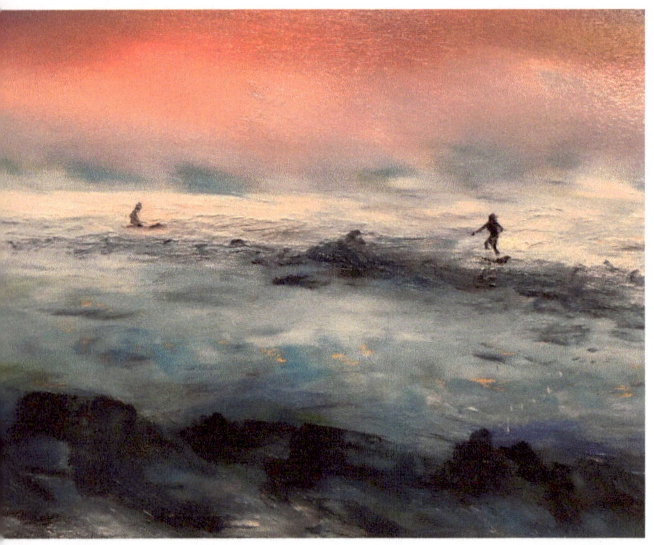

Once the upper wave has been established, go back to the wave at the bottom of the painting and begin to block in its crest too.

I used a palette knife for all of this, allowing plenty of texture. Small dabbing motions with a loaded palette knife produce lovely fresh droplets.

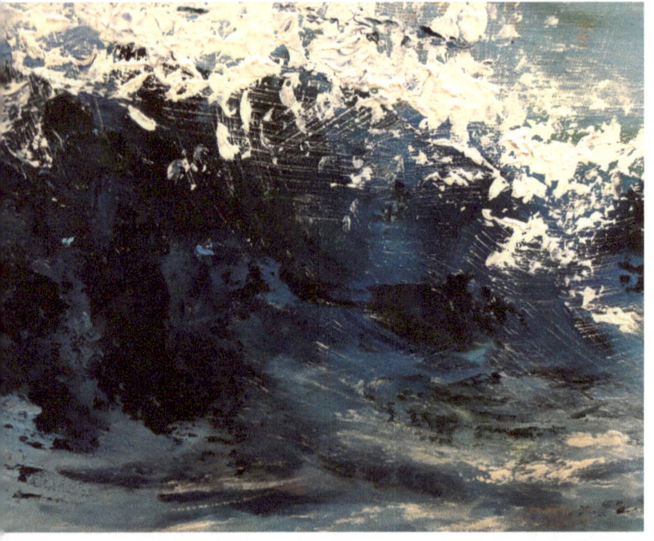

When the whole wave crest has been blocked in, soften again with a fan brush but also go back and make sure the undertones of the rising wave are sufficiently defined.

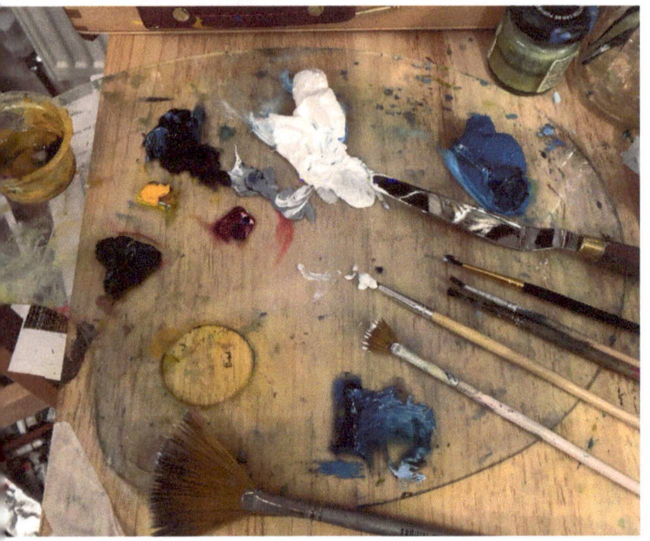

French Ultramarine, Cerulean Blue, Sap Green and Payne's Grey are my staple mix here. Don't mix too thoroughly; let the individual colours show through for more depth and lustre. Here you can also see the selection of fine-headed brushes I used to sketch in the surfers.

Finally, I went back over the central section of sea between the two waves and added just a hint of the threatening red of the sky so that sea and sky were still connected by reflection…

And it is complete…

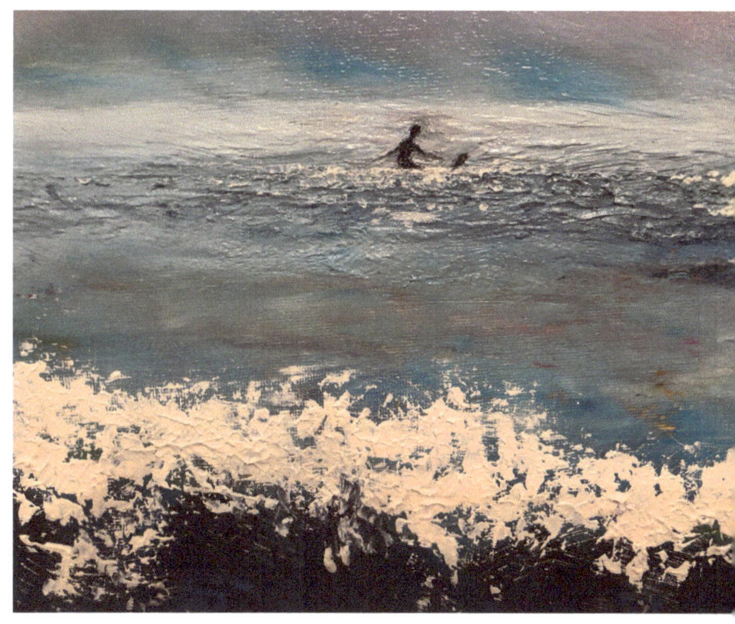

I called it 'Cresting Waves'.

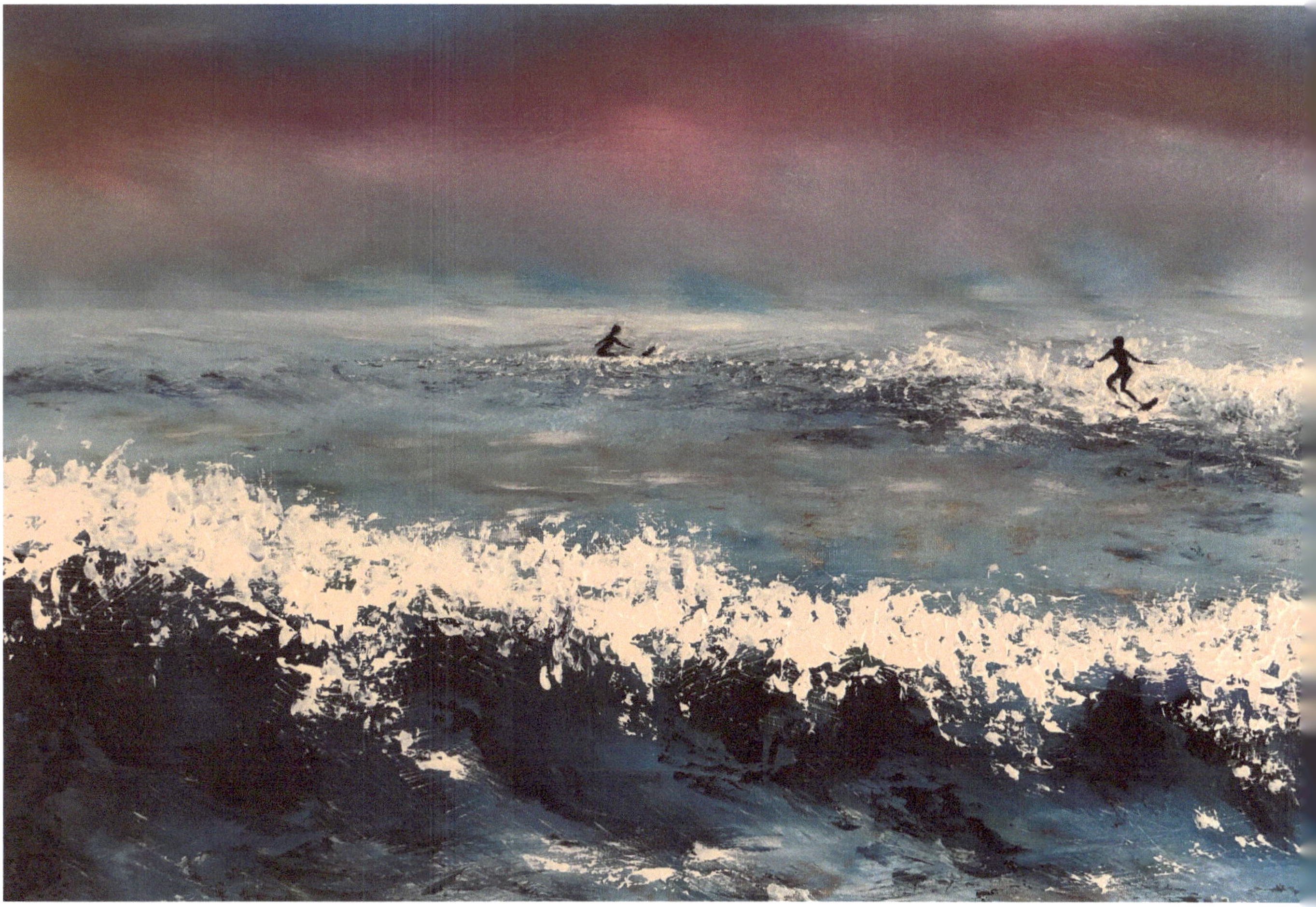

Cresting Waves

Inspired by surfers at Bondi Beach

He steadies and skims,
Toes digging in tight to the board as it lifts, curves,
Glissées through to the highest point.

Bursting from the outer edge of the cresting wave,
He is victorious.
Invincible.
She follows, skimming his wake,
Glorying in his triumphant arc,
Nestling into the furrow he has ploughed.
Two cresting waves.

Nothing can topple them,
except time, and tide, and frailty.
But there is none of that in them today.
The wave is with them,
Propelling them on;
A promise of victory.

And even as their dominance of the sea is defeated,
Tumbling headlong in a crash of spume and spray and upended board,
Their passage is still luminescent with hope;
Bright and bold and fluid.
For they are cresting waves, arcing from one to the other,
Rolling to the shore and dissolving gently in a tangle of limbs at the water's edge,
To rise again together, as the tide teases them back into its flow.

As I travelled around Australia and New Zealand in 2018, I also became very aware of the dangers and depths of mystery to the sea. 2018 itself ended with saddening news of many deaths from a tsunami in Indonesia, and for me it struck home far more emphatically than it would normally have done because I had only recently seen the tsunami evacuation signs on the waterfront on The Bay of Islands…

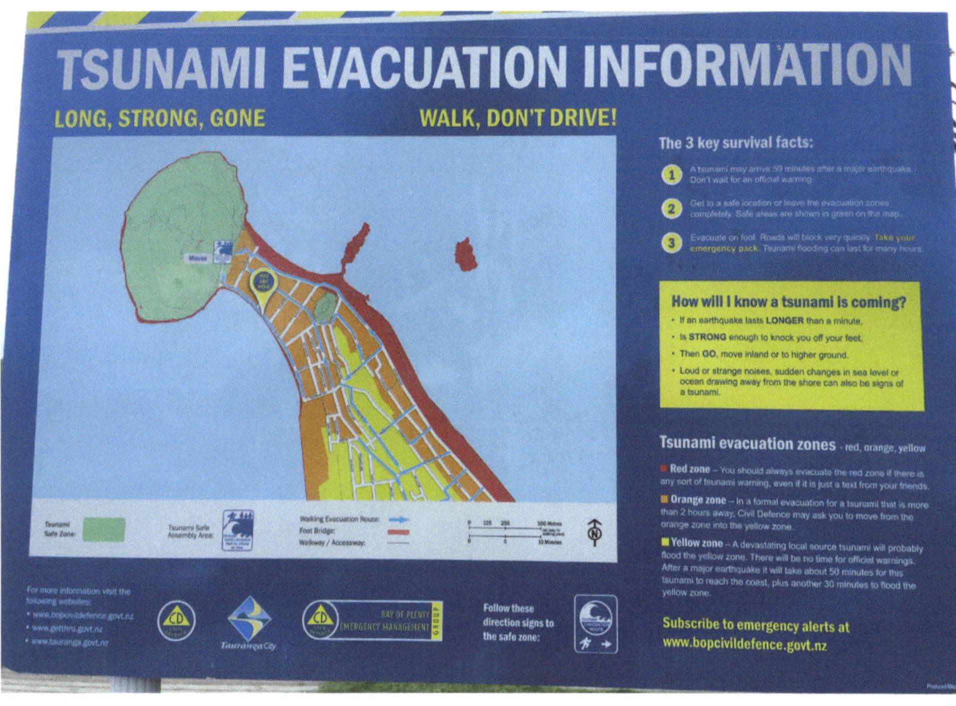

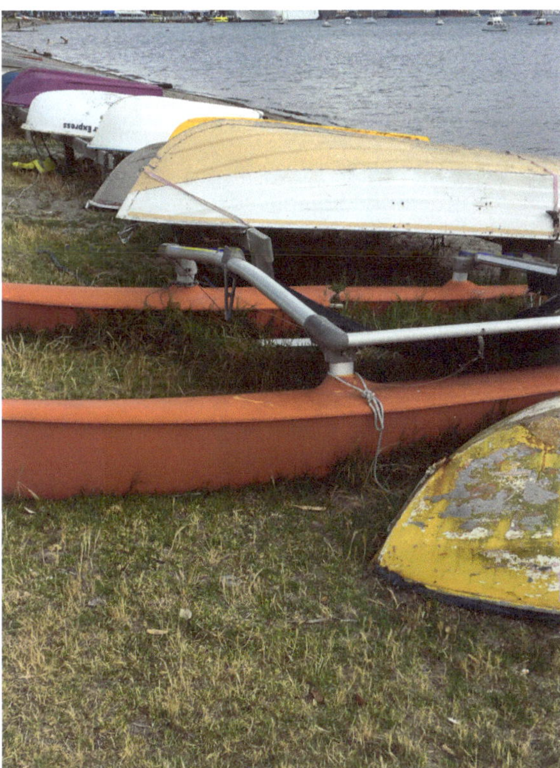

… an otherwise deceptively peaceful place.

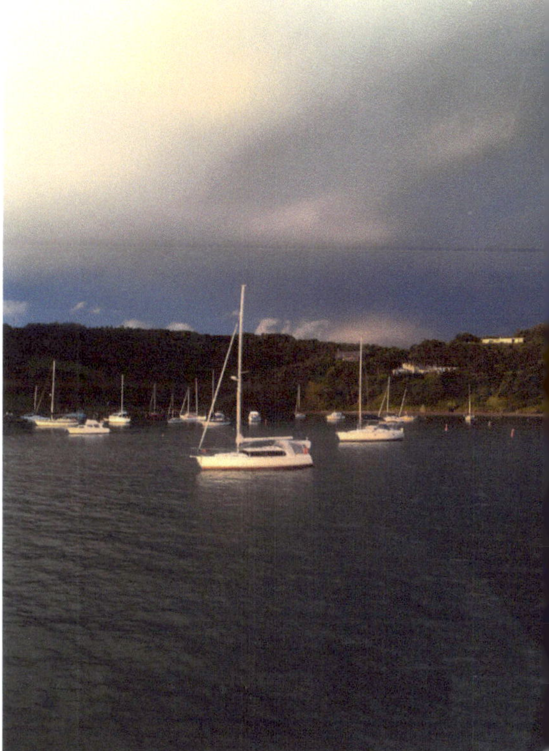

It reminded me of this, written some while ago for an – as yet – unpublished thriller trilogy:

The Wave

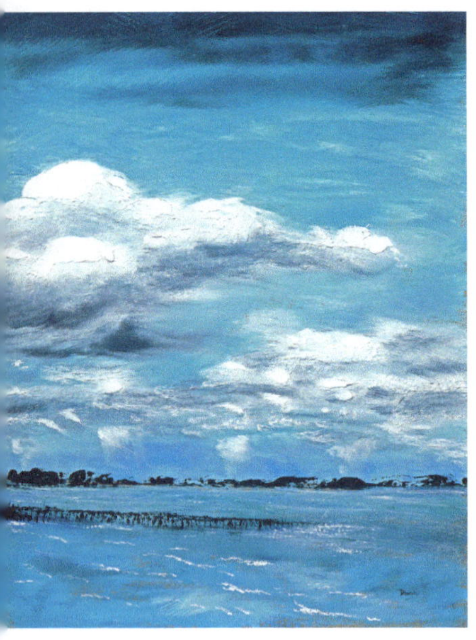

Lazily she scanned the horizon, chin in hands, elbows sinking into the soft tickle of grass as she stretched out full length atop her vantage point. If she tipped her head right back to stare at the sky, she could almost touch the downy white of the puffball clouds bobbing above her, but that was tiring. She let her eyes drift back down to the coastline instead, following the movement of the gently rippling swell and the hovering gulls as they balanced on the air currents.

It smelt of dry earth and hot sun up here. Down there it would smell of salt and sand and summer. She let her breath out so completely she could have been empty of everything except the rhythm of the waves as they caressed the shore. She always loved that sensation – empty, and yet full of nothing – the nothing that came before *something*…

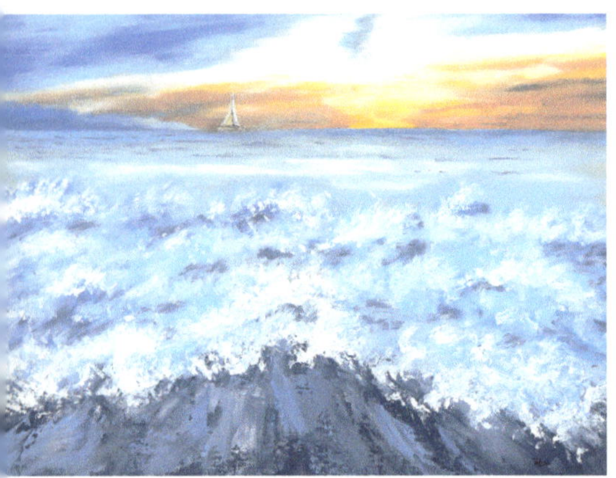

Time passed – minutes, maybe hours. She didn't care. It was too perfect being nowhere with nothing inside her on a day like today. She yawned. *Sleepyhead, sitting in the sun …* The words of a song someone used to sing to me. She smiled. Probably Aunt Kay. She liked singing. Far below, the sand stretched into oblivion, gold against azure; and the surf still swept steadily up the beach, and back down again. Idly she watched it move back and forth, barely noticing the pattern of blue and gold shifting as the tide rolled in, until the change was too apparent to miss. More gold, less blue.

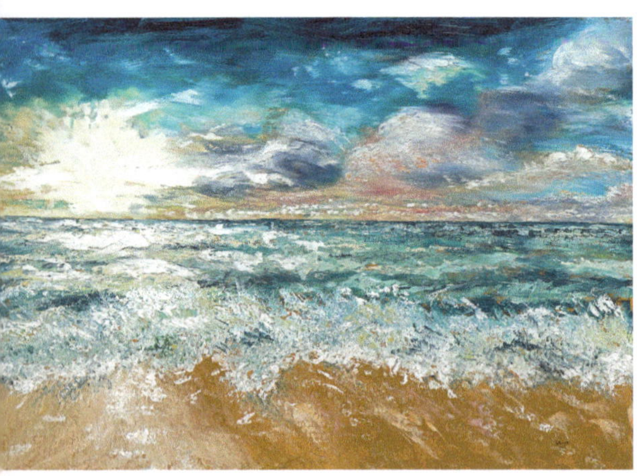

A lot more gold, in fact – lengthening far into the distance. She focussed then, suddenly conscious something wasn't right. There was too much gold; far too much. She frowned. How could the tide go out that quickly, disappearing like it was being sucked back into the sea?

Now the previously golden strip was dark and claggy like the earthy clay paste she used to make mud castles from, and the shoreline ragged with seaweed. The air was sharp too; the tang of salty spray invading the previously sweet, dry aroma of sun and earth. She breathed in sharply, surprised, filling her lungs with the change. There was a sour taste of brine on her lips as the sea gulls broke formation and screeched frenziedly overhead. They wheeled away, calling urgently, shrill and insistent. *Look, look.* Head spinning, she followed their somersaulting into the distance, and looked. Her bewildered gaze ended abruptly there. She stared out to sea, open-mouthed.

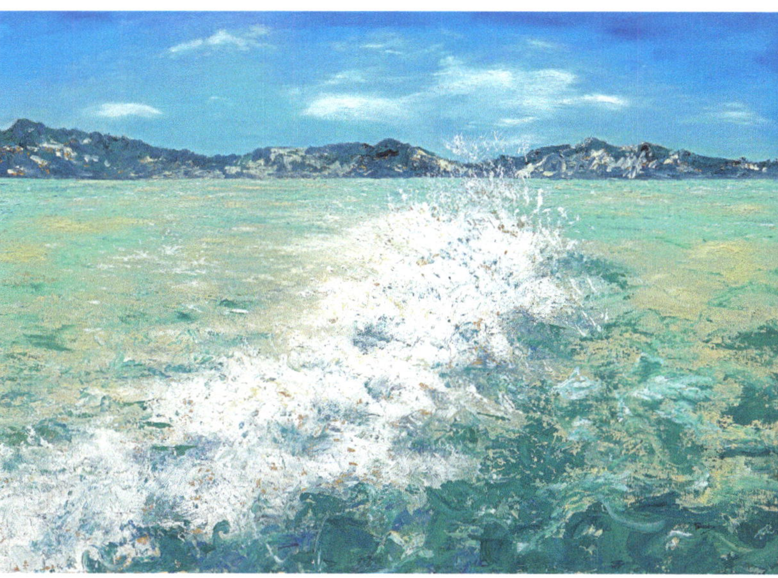

The horizon was bulging, blistering. Along the faint white line that separated sea from sky there was now an impatient fizzing. On the beach far below her, the summer revellers had also noticed the change, staring out to sea, pointing, then calling to each other. They gathered in excited groups, marvelling at the contracting tide and the simmering horizon. Children left their sand castles and kicked delightedly at the multitude of shells they could now see. They ran to collect them in their buckets, carrying their precious hauls back to promising masterpieces, giggling and calling in high-pitched trills. Mothers deserted their basecamps of picnic baskets and checked blankets to venture onto the vast expanse of mud-sand, their white winter legs and bright floral costumes turning them into exotic flowers on spindly stems. The shoreline became a crowd of curious bystanders, waiting for the parade to arrive. She scrambled to her feet to join them, teetering far above them on her rocky promontory with its patchy grass cushion. For the first time, she wondered where she was – and how she'd got here. But where and how became irrelevant in the face of the strange turn in the tide. Swelling obscenely out of the bubbling horizon; The Wave.

Someone screamed – it might even have been her.

Then more screams, shouts; panic replacing curiosity – the signal for the previously trans-fixed crowds to turn, stumbling desperately up the beach, barging and trampling. A small boy tripped and fell, crying frantically for his mother. A woman hesitated, staring in terror as the mass of water loomed in the distance. Too far away for her to hear, the woman's words should have been lost in the roar of the

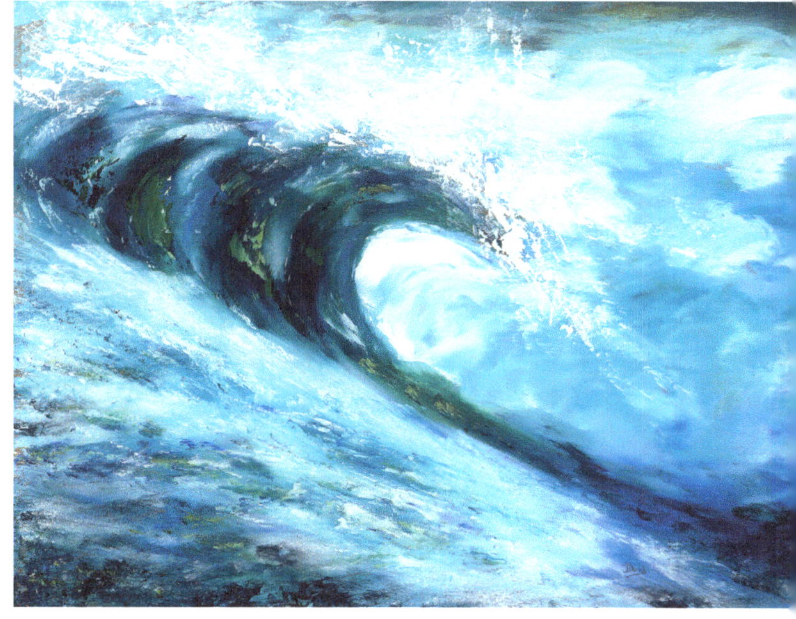

oncoming deluge and yet she could hear and see everything clearly, as if she was down there too. Her ears sang with the rush of The Wave and the beat of her blood. She watched, numb with horror, as the woman grabbed the child up, hugging him close as if that would save him. She watched, sweating with fear, as they struggled up the beach, bawling at them to urge them on even though they couldn't hear her, her fists clenched and palms pricking, knowing they couldn't make it.

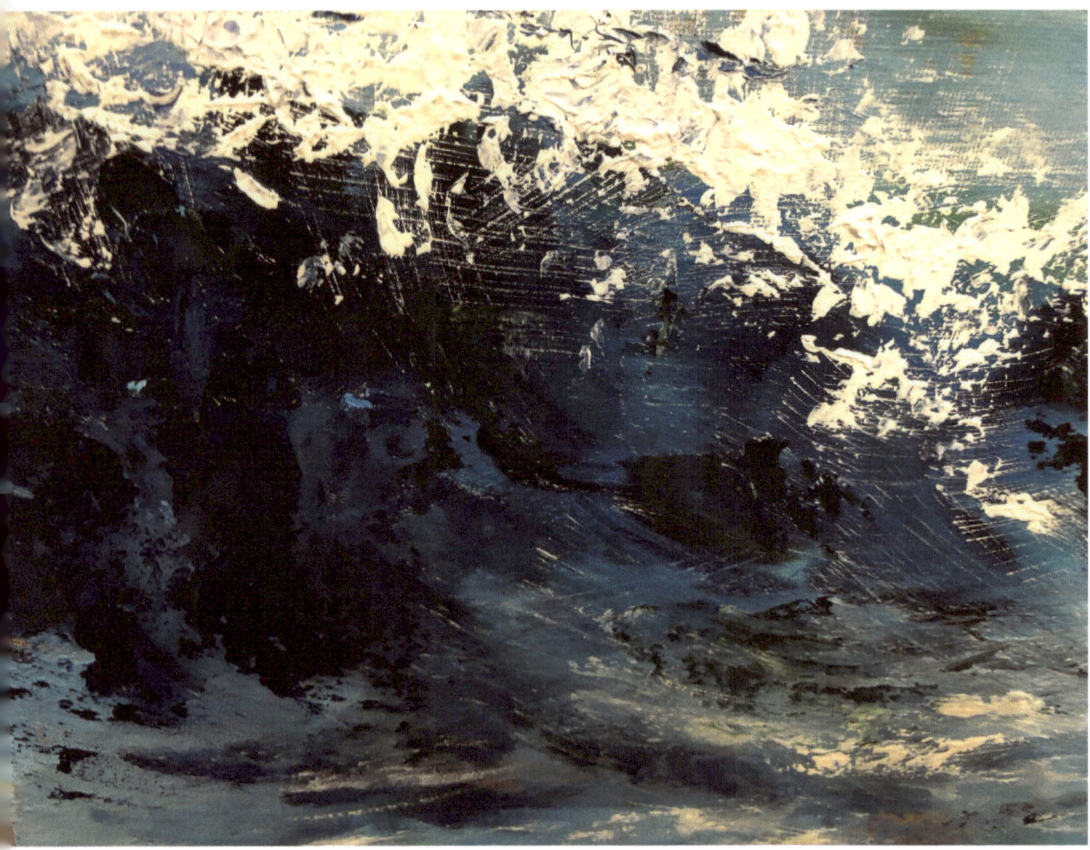

Fore-runners tumbled onto the emptied shore-line behind them, crashing and rolling as they hit the sand barrier. She screamed for the stragglers to run, faster, harder; don't stop! They fled, too slowly, as The Wave swept in, demolishing abandoned family picnics and engulfing the fleeing swarm of ants that once were people. She sobbed, but the sound was lost in the thunder of The Wave, shaking the ground under her feet and throwing her to her knees. She struggled upright and breathlessly scoured the beach for the woman and crying child, but they were long gone in the spume. Her heart pounded and her skin crawled. As the gull's screeches turned to human cries of terror, the roar of the tumbling water became the sound of the world drowning beneath a dark tide of chaos.

Sometimes the sea is serene, sometimes mysterious; always it is hypnotic.

That is why I paint it.

PART 2: GETTING STARTED - EQUIPMENT

P erceiving, portraying and painting are all subjective skills. We all 'see' things differently. We all 'like' different ways of projecting images. Some like fine, 'photographic' art. Others respond to impressionistic work, or abstract images.

There is no right or wrong way to paint, but there are techniques you can learn and deploy and make your own, adapting them to your own style, and there are equipment and materials that make it more possible to do so – as well as essential to even get started. Here are some of my recommendations:

Studio equipment:

Easel – mine is a beautiful beast bought off eBay! Here it is in pristine condition.

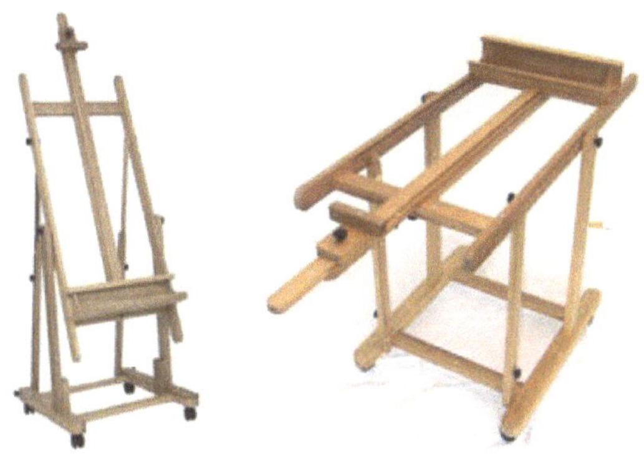

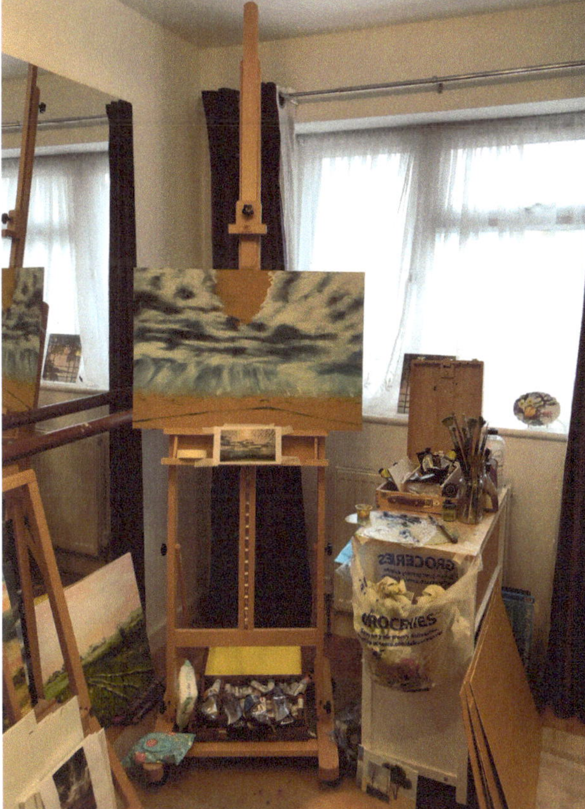

It looks like this in practice …

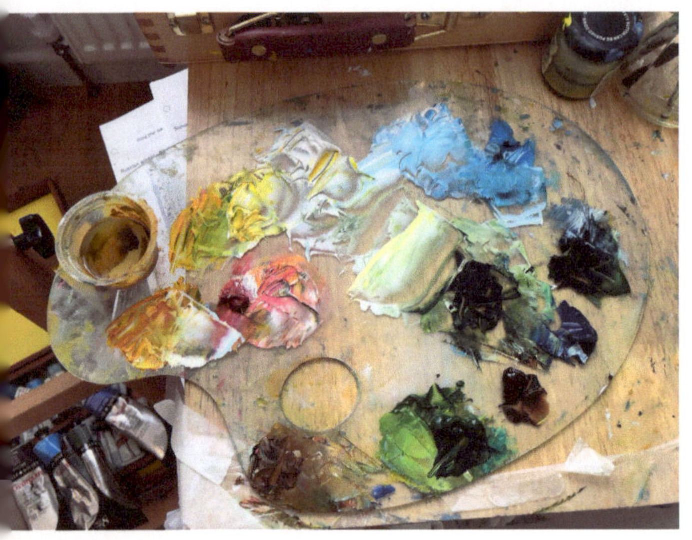

- A stool - if you like to sit. Personally, I prefer to stand so I can easily step back and consider what I've been working on. Distance is a great leveller.

- A glass or clear acrylic palette. Mine's clear acrylic; ideal if you're clumsy!

- Brushes: filberts, rounds, fan and fine detail brushes – lots of suggestions in the brushes section below.

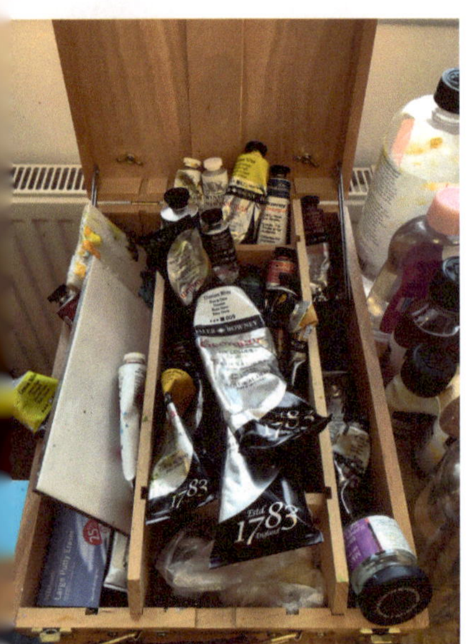

- Palette knife for mixing (and applying if you paint like me). Suggestions are given below, and of course palette knife painting is a technique all of its own so if you find you enjoy applying paint with the palette knife, then there are plenty of palette knives to try out.

- Canvas or canvas board to paint on.

- Paint; the basic requirements are detailed below. You don't need this much, but it's always fun experimenting as your collection grows.

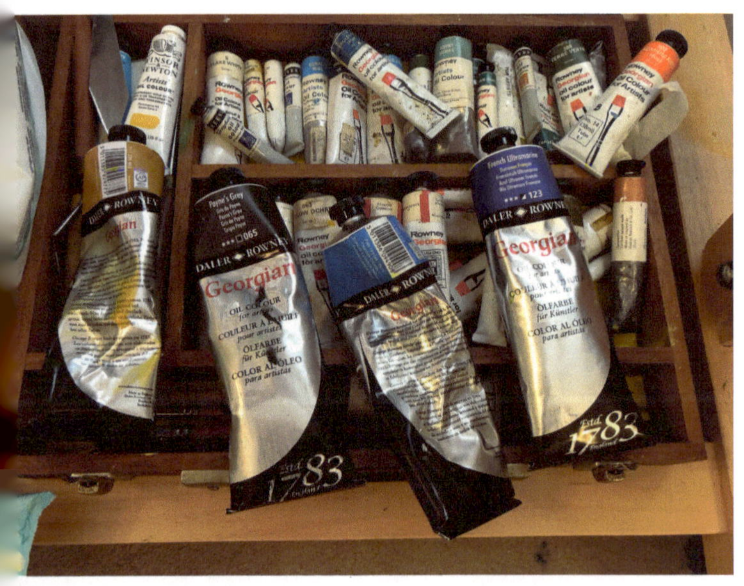

- Medium and solvent for thinning and cleaning, again all detailed below.

Sundries:

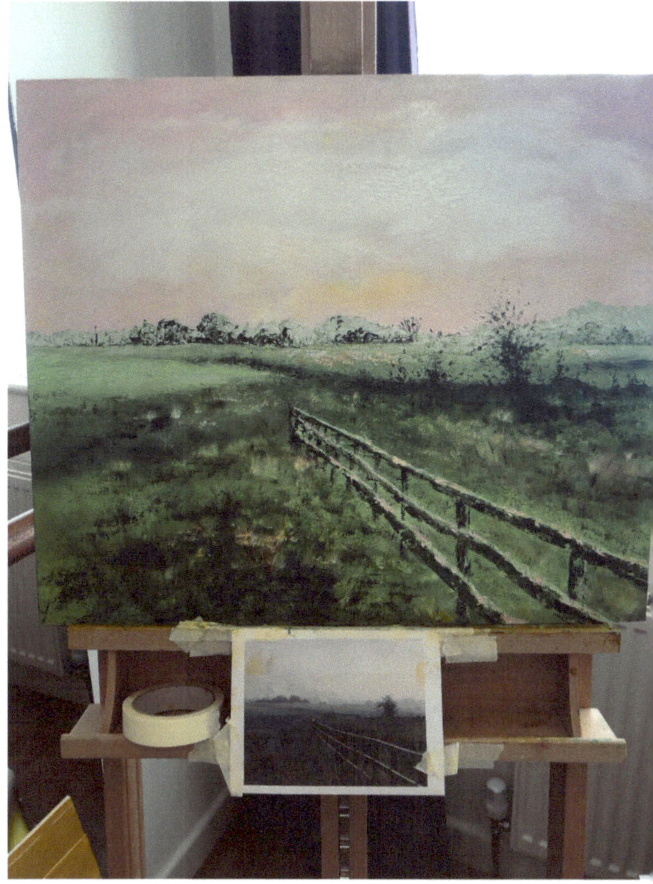

- An apron, or your special painting clothes. Mine are some old jeans, a miscellany of old tee-shirts and tops, and a fine lawn shirt that didn't make it to Peru with me but is wonderful for covering up a bikini top and avoiding sunburn when I'm painting outside in the summer.

- Soft rags for rubbing under-painting – those old PJ's you really should throw out are wonderful for this, cut or ripped into squares.

- Masking tape for fixing images you are working from and for taping a rubbish bag to your working area.

- Plastic ruler (for straight horizons and buildings).

- Jars for brushes.

- Cleaning materials for hands – vegetable fluid, kitchen roll, tissues, wipes.

- Plastic bags for rubbish – and there's a lot of it by the time you've cleaned palettes, palette knives brushes and hands, believe me!

For special effects:

There are a variety of ways of creating special effects – either with use of specific brushes, or with other materials. These are some I use:

- Tissue paper
- Blending brushes
- Sponges
- Stippling brushes
- Fan brushes

Canvas and Board:

I paint a lot on canvas board, but even so I prefer specific types to others. Surface texture varies enormously, and some canvas boards are less forgiving, some more absorbent. I prefer Jacksons Premium Cotton Canvas Board, or Loxley Acid-free Cotton Canvas Board, or Winsor and Newton Artist's Canvas Board. I'm not so keen on Daler Board for oils, although 'Shotover Hill looking

South' is painted on Daler Board. You can also paint on canvas – more give – and on MDF as long as you prepare the surface with good quality gesso.

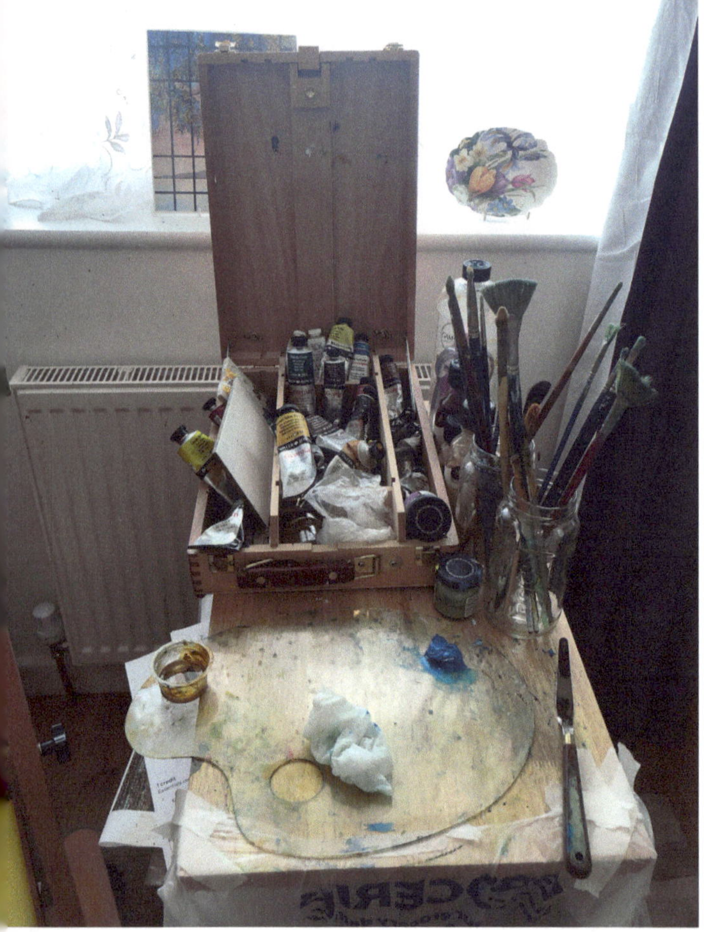

Brushes:

Standard are:
Filbert sizes 8, 6, 4 and 2
Round size 2, 0

My fan brushes are Winsor and Newton 'Winton' series, Pro Arte Series F Fan brush, number 50686513 and Daler D55 'Dalon'. I also use Jackson's Silverline Watercolour Brush Series 989: Fan Size 10 a lot, even though it's intended for watercolour painting. It gives the most beautiful softening finish, evening out brush strokes even after using a fan brush. I have one other tiny fan brush, the smallest you can get, basically used for watercolour painting but it's invaluable for very fine detail, so play around until you find what suits you best.

Filbert brushes have a rounded flat tip and a flat ferrule.

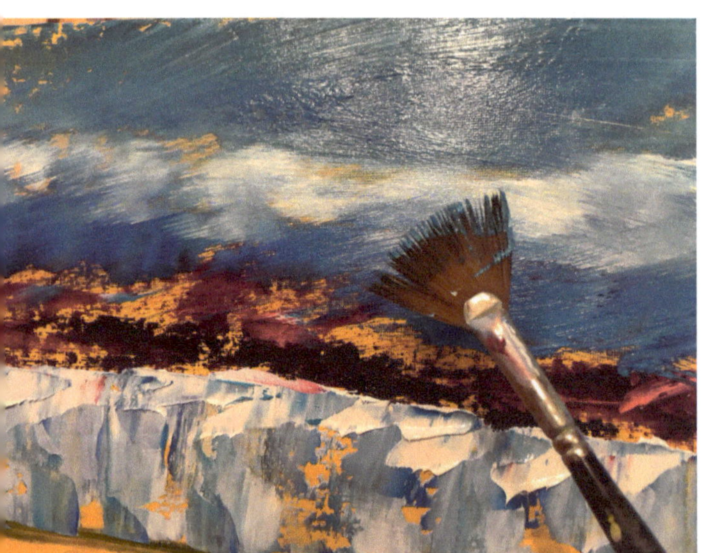

Round brushes have a pointed tip and a round ferrule.

The best quality bristle brushes are Chungking Bristle, and some good ones to use as basics are:
Filbert Handover Chungking Studio hog's hair brush series 314.
Round Handover Chungking Studio hog's hair brush series 316.
System 3 series SY278 short flat synthetic brush.

For stippling, I use:
Winsor and Newton 'Winton' Abanico.
Daler B84 'Bristlewhite'.

Palette knives

I have a huge variety – courtesy of my lovely
father, who was a stand-out oil painter.

A lot of the detail in 'The Ridgeway in Winter,
early morning' was added with my trusty
paint-mixing and applying palette knife (far
right-hand side of the photograph), as old as the
hills and one of my father's favourites. Similar to
this is an RGM palette knife, number 105. This,
plus a back-up like an RGM RPK1, should see
you well-served to start with.

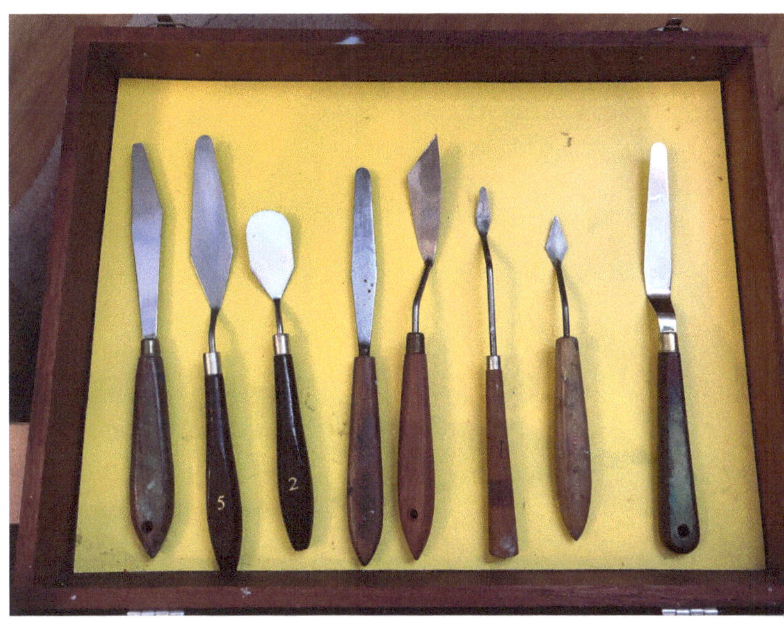

Mediums and solvents:

Mediums thin paint and make it dry quicker. You don't want to use it a lot, but for fine detail it is good. It
is also useful when under-painting so you only add a thin layer, easy to 'smudge'. Mediums I use for this
or for fine detail work are Winsor and Newton Liquin Fine detail, and for general use, Liquin. You can
also use Gamblin Galkyd, made in the USA but available from UK art suppliers. Liquin is a little glossier
and more accessible overall. Mediums speed up drying too and enable paint to be more translucent.

Solvents are for cleaning brushes. Do not use solvents for thinning or when painting. Winsor and
Newton Sansodor are virtually odourless and low in toxicity. Gamblin Gamsol is totally odourless and
also low in toxicity. I tend to use Gamblin.

You can clean your palette off with vegetable oil and tissue/ kitchen roll. Kitchen roll is a staple when
painting; for cleaning palettes, brushes and you! Clean your hands with baby oil, or baby wipes. To clean
your brushes properly:

- Wipe the excess paint off first on kitchen roll.
- Have two jars containing your chosen solvent, one for the first general wash to get most of
  the paint off, and one for the second and final clean. Wipe excess solvent and paint off on
  an old towel between each wash. After the second wash, your brush shouldn't leave paint on
  the towel. If it does, repeat the process. Brushes only stay usable if properly cleaned after use.
- Always clean your brushes after use and between colour changes. Wrecked brushes = no
  painting!

Paint:

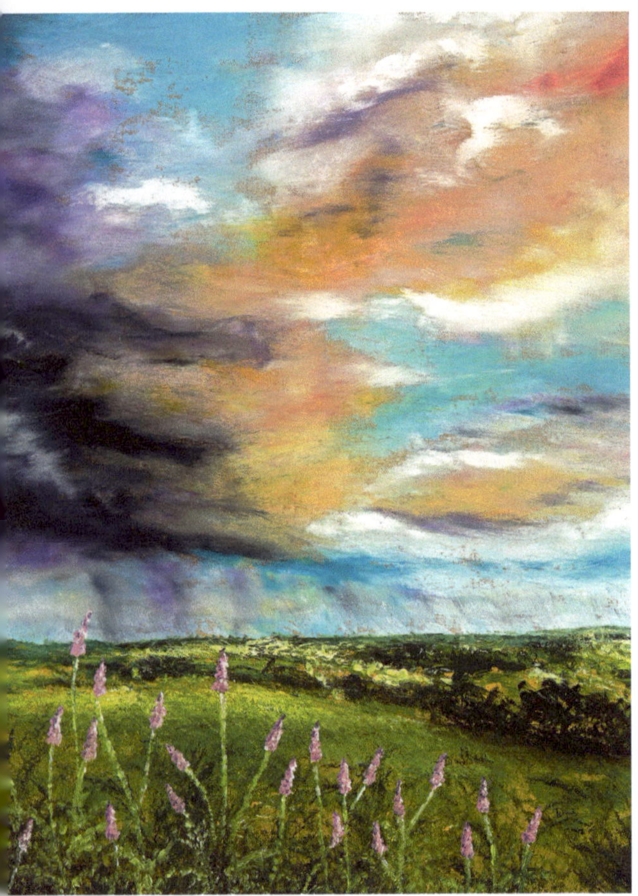

Personally, I use Daler Rowney Georgian oil colour, supplemented by Winsor and Newton Artist's Oil Colour. It isn't cheap, so when first starting oil painting, I suggest you use something like a starter set, e.g. Winton, then gradually replace your paints with better quality 'Artist's' colours as and when they are used up. Cheaper paint has less pigment in it and more binder so long-term it won't hold its tint as well as more expensive paint. Artist's oils also have better viscosity so are nicer to use, but get to know your colours, your palette, your style and your technique first, invest later.

Staple colours I suggest are:
Titanium White
Lemon Yellow
Cadmium (sometimes called 'Chrome') Yellow
Alizarin Crimson
Cadmium Red
Ultramarine Blue
Phtahlo Blue (pronounced 'thaylo')
Yellow Ochre
Raw Umber
Burnt Sienna
Burnt Umber
Ivory Black
I also use a lot of – in fact, often paint entirely with:
Sap Green
Cerulean Blue
Phtahlo Grey
Permanent Rose
Cadmium Yellow Deep

I often keep to a limited palette, something I first learn to do when watercolour painting. If you look at the section on colour palettes and colour wheels below, you'll see you can make almost any colour from a very limited bunch and it's well-worth experimenting to see what + what = what. Even with a limited palette you can achieve a vast range of colour, such as in 'Pinks', above.

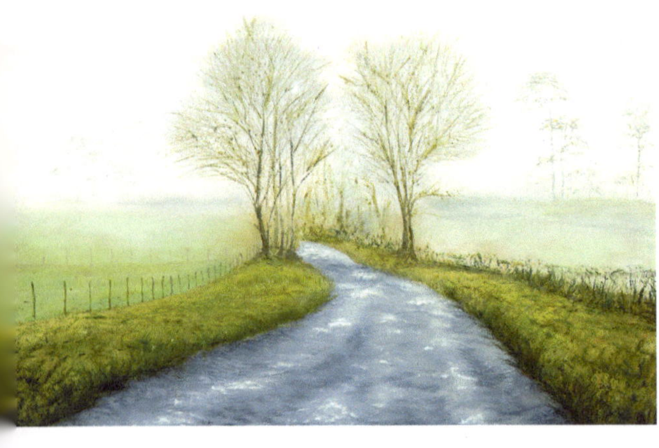

Or you can stay pastel and translucent, like in this winter scene.

PART 3: LAND AND SKYSCAPES

As much as the sea fascinates me, so do skies. Amazing, surreal, prophetic, serene; every day they are different, and yet every day they are the same too. We see other worlds in skies; places that might be, or other realms that could be. That's why we look to the sky so often, and all the characters in our dreams look there too – for inspiration, for hope, for rescue … Our imagination runs wild when we look up to the sky and reach for something more than ourselves. What do you see when you stare up into the sky? I see possibilities.

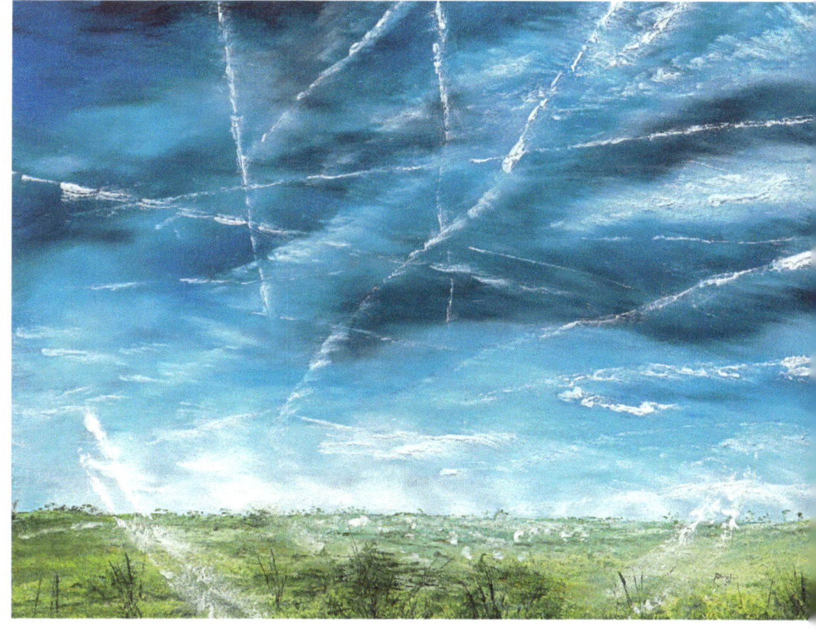

Sky staring,
I crane my neck until it reaches
The foamy clouds.
The sky is an ocean,
Flowing into space.
Upside down, it cascades over me,
Drowning me in blue,
Filling my head with imagination bubbles.
Pop.
I am sky staring,
As the sky spreads over my head, and into my dreams,
And the ideas tumble around me like raindrops…

The painting below is painted from a photograph taken by an amazing photographer called Tim Turan, whilst at the Common People festival in Oxford in 2018. Sadly, Common People is no more as it went into administration shortly afterwards, but I still think it captures the way I feel when I stare up into the sky better than any words can. It's a symbol of celebration, as well as inspiration.

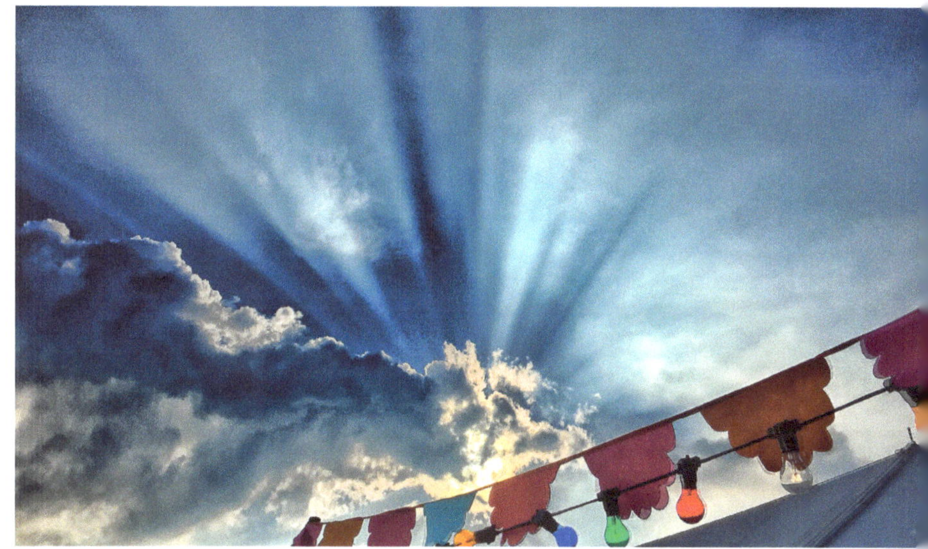

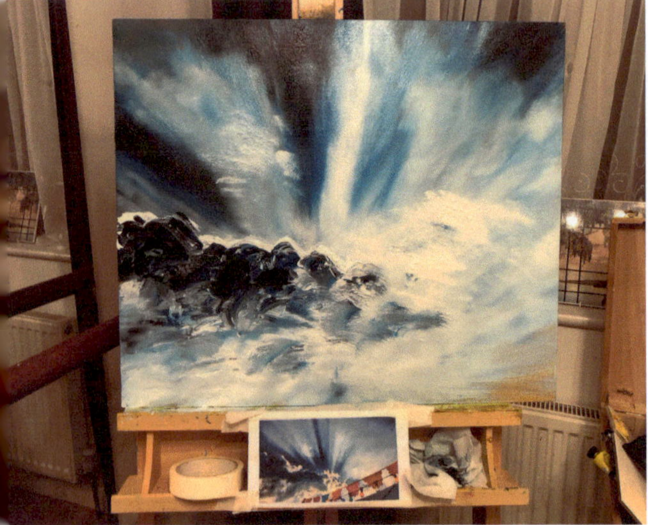

Painting skies can be so easy – and so tough.

The Common People painting took me several goes, and a lot of paint scraping before it went from this…

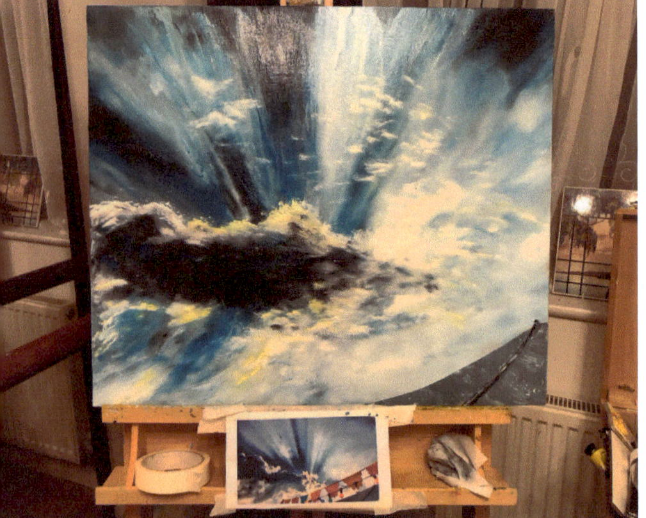

Via this …

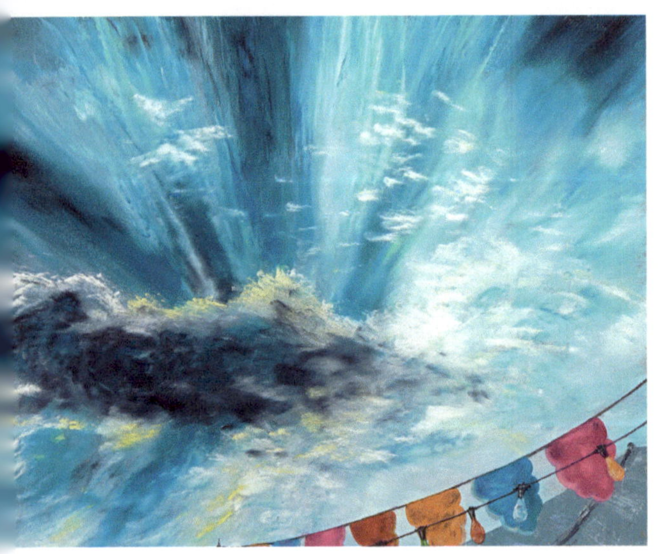

To how it ended up.

Painting skies is all about capturing the essence of them, the range of colour that is within a sky – like this one.

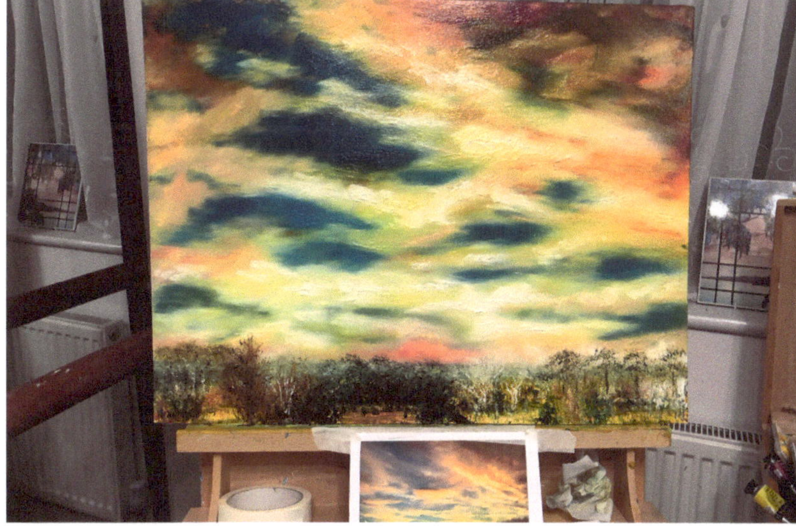

Don't believe skies are like that? Check this one out, then – taken standing on my front doorstep whilst I was painting the one above!

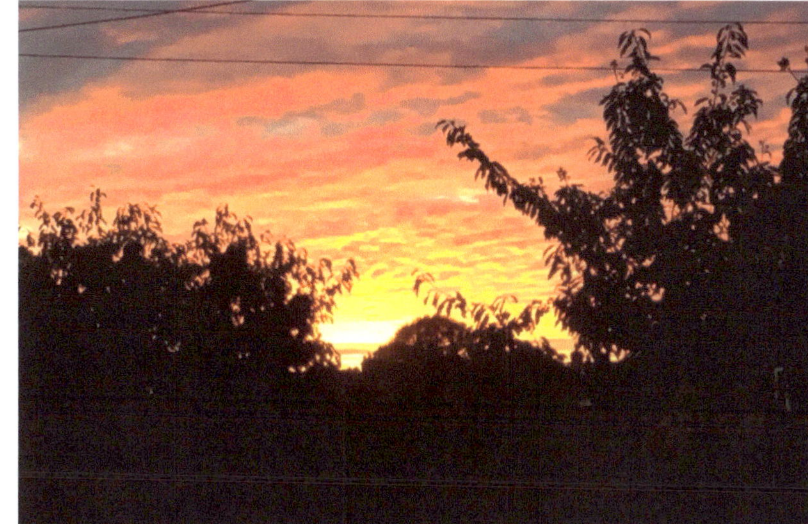

So, lets paint a sky – and a tricky one at that, because what's life without a challenge? This seemed a good one at the time …

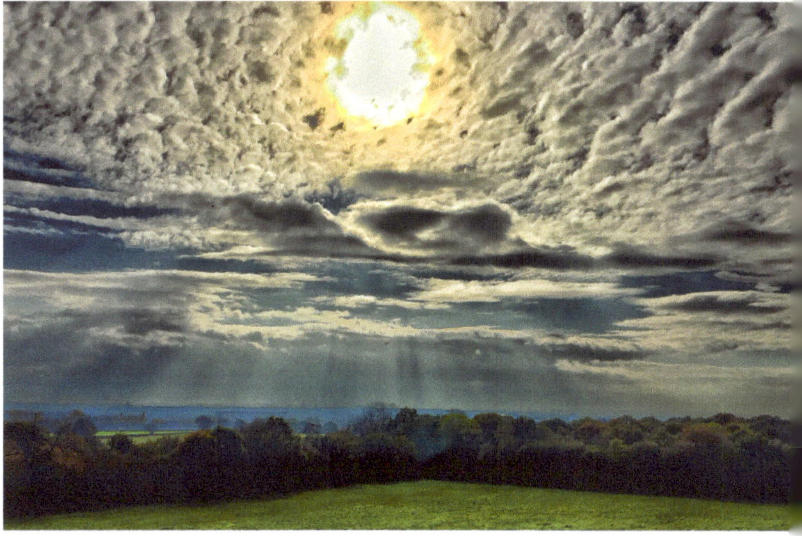

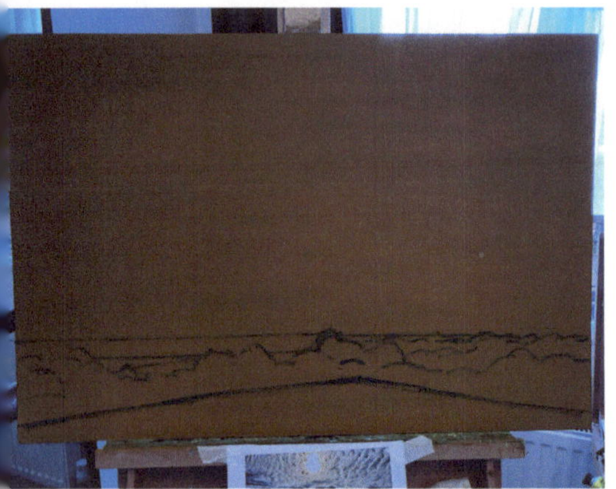

I started with sketching in the horizon remembering those golden proportions we look for in the Rule of Thirds (go forward to Part 4) so the horizon itself is about 1/3 the way up the painting.

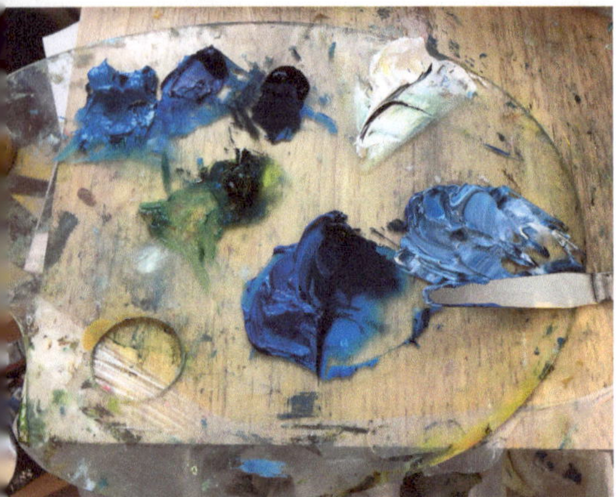

My palette was based around Cerulean Blue, French Ultramarine, Payne's Grey and Titanium White – far and away my favourites for skies.

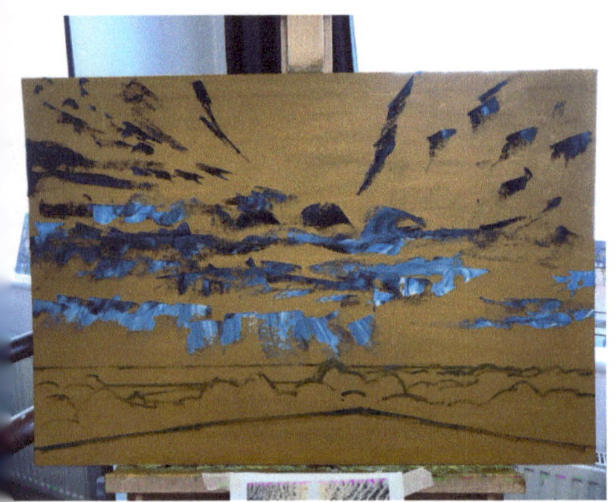

One difference with the way I tackled this painting was that the oil board I was using wasn't my usual type – and unlike the palette – not my favourite. I roughed in the darks before the white this time, taking into account the texture of the board, absorbability and coverage. The smoother the board or canvas, the better the coverage, so concentrate on areas if you have a board or canvas with a rough texture as you won't get the 'spread' you would otherwise get with a sweep of the palette knife.

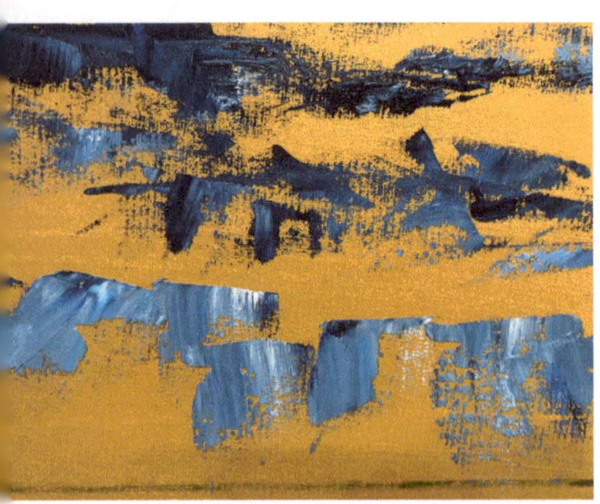

You can see the coarseness of the texture here, but varying textures is good as it encourages versatility and flexibility in your painting. Never be afraid to try something new – or difficult; it develops your capabilities and refines and adapts techniques. You become a better painter for having risen to challenges.

When I mix paint, I use a palette knife and mix enough quantity on my palette to cover sufficient areas to work on large-scale, as well as retain some of the paint to colour match later. Inevitably there will be times when you either mix too much or too little, but overall, I would tend to mix too little as it is easy to colour match, even if it takes a little while and is somewhat painstaking. Mixing too much is a waste, and whilst you might be able to conserve it on another palette – or a plain white tile, covered in clingfilm and then frozen (great little tip for saving surplus paint, that), you still run the risk of using a colour that isn't quite right in the future, for the sake of using up the paint.

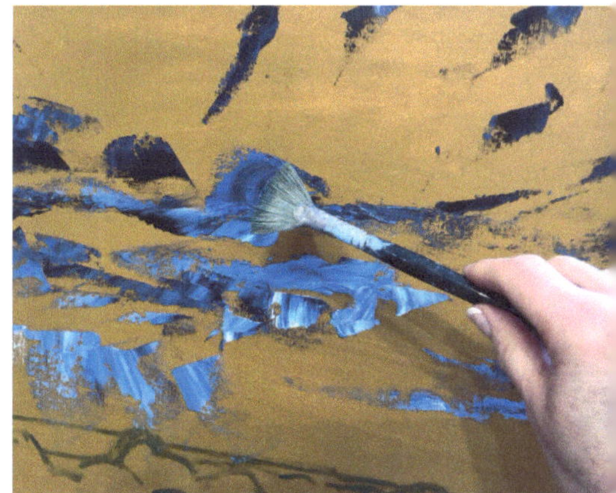

If you make a note of the pigments and quantities used, it shouldn't be too difficult to create the same shade again – and of course, I do not mix to oblivion. That means I don't mix my colours until they are all one colour. If you look at the image above of the texture, you will see the paint is texturised too – it has shades within it. Nothing you see in the real world is one colour alone so why use one colour? Blending will sort out any over-dark or light areas, and mimic nature.

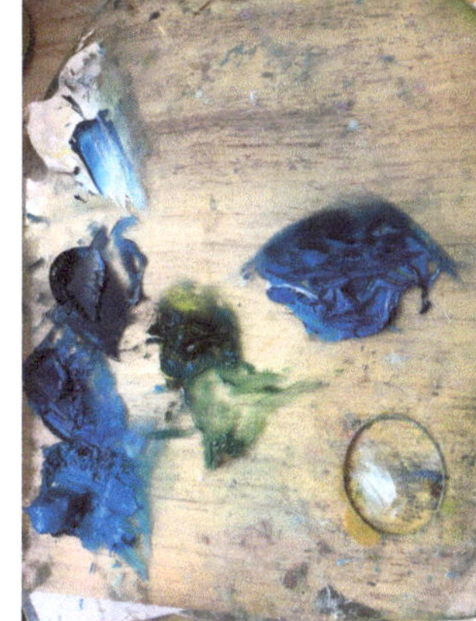

Once the main darks are blocked in, I'm working to add in the lighter areas of cloud, knowing that when I blend these colours, they will merge and the darks become far softer, so don't worry if it seems too light or too dark at this stage.

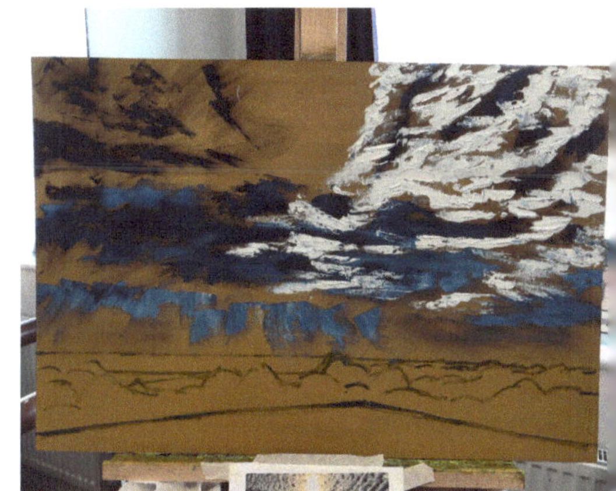

Note there is already some tonal difference in the paint I have applied, so when you know there is an area of – say – mid-blue – do work it in as you go, alongside the light and dark areas, just don't get hide-bound about putting in exactly the colour you think is there. Remember Part 2? What you think is there, is only what you *think* is there …

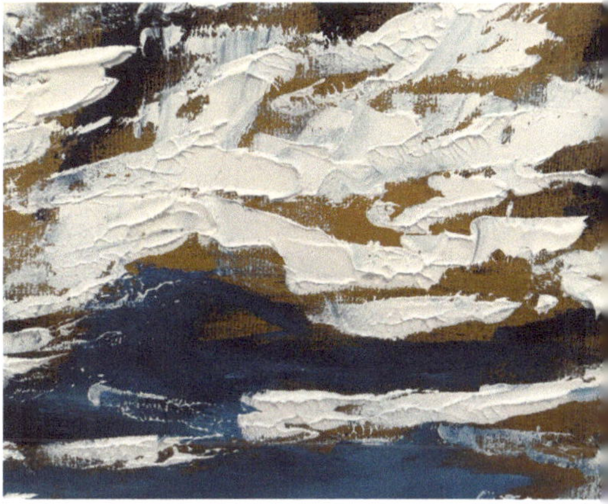

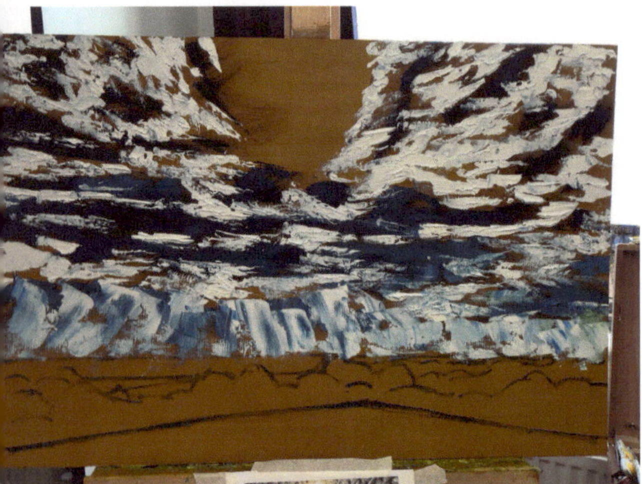

And here it is with the whole sky tonally blocked, but unblended – apart from the lower edge to the clouds where I know the light is spilling down in what look like spotlights. It is a little surreal and yet we know it was how the light was being perceived by the onlooker from the photograph. Truth *is* stranger than fiction, huh?

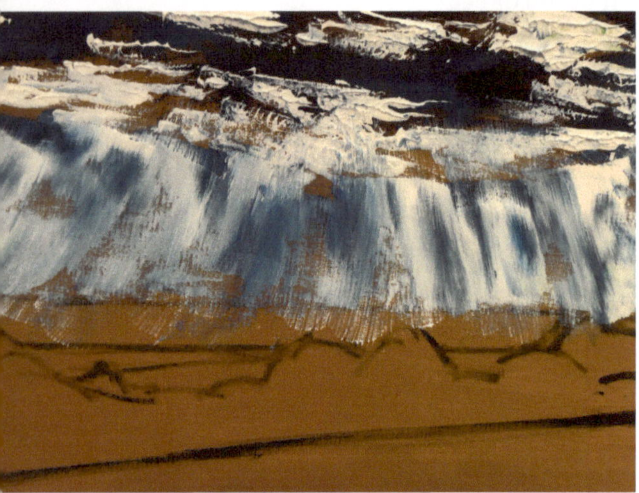

Next, I work on this area as a priority because I will need to be able to develop a clean line along the underside of the lower bank of clouds and I can only do this by sweeping the brush along their edge. Therefore, I need the lower area to be completed first.

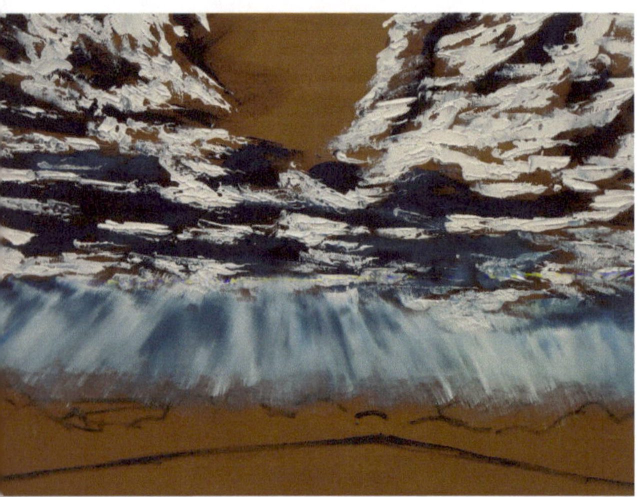

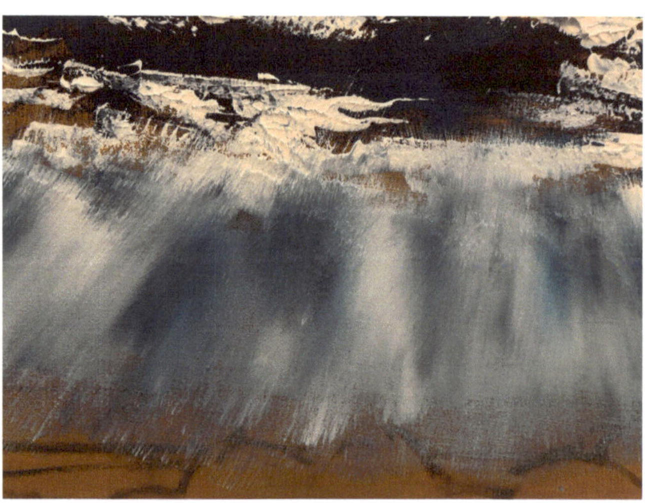

It's quite effective once complete, having used downward brush strokes and my Silverline brush to really soften and smooth the light beams.

The upper clouds are still rough and unblended so now I will start to run them into each other with either my Pro Arte series F or Daler fan brushes.

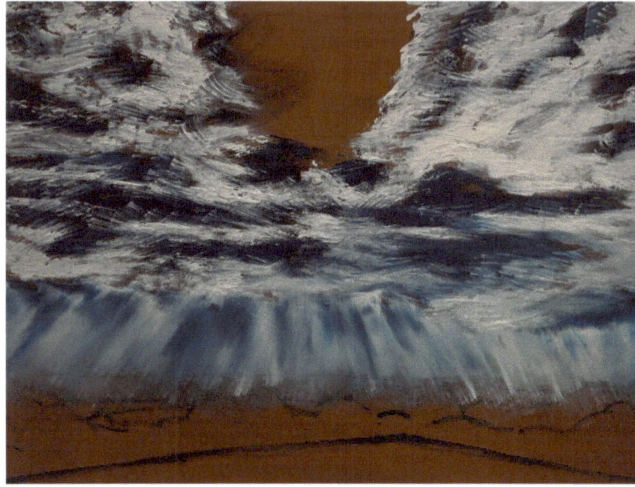

The effect initially is rough and messy, but the more you work – gently – on the paint, the better the tones will work together, until you can achieve a sense of blurring of one tone into another. It is this that gives the clouds their dense formation.

These are stages in cloud blending…

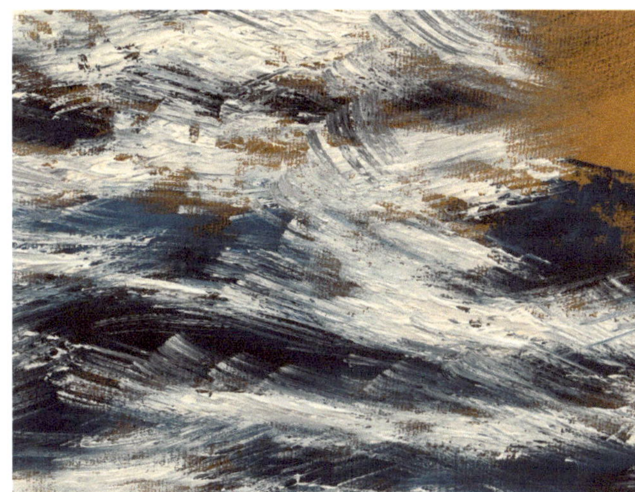

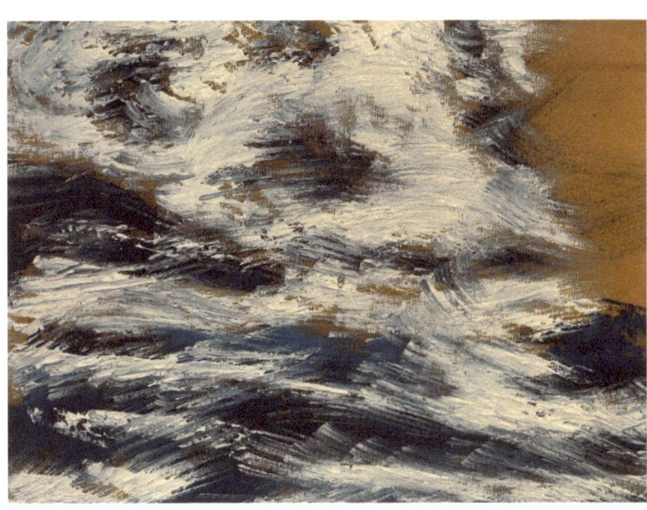

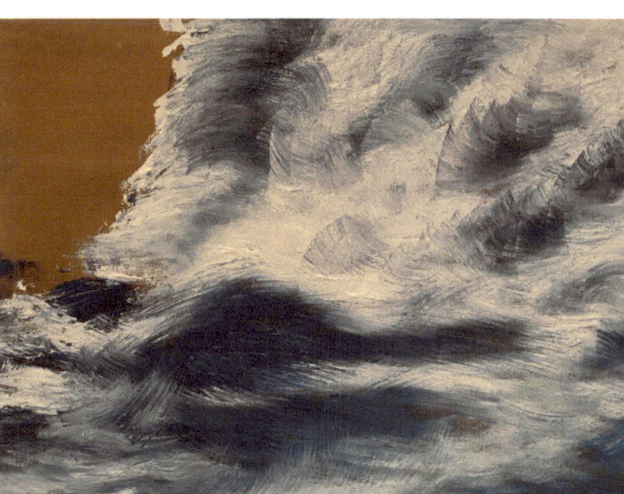

And in the next image you can see the difference between the section that has been worked on and the section with its tonal blocking untouched.

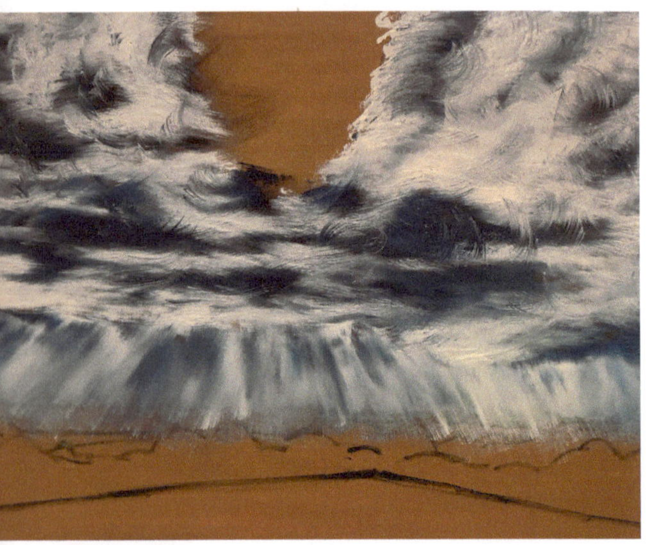

Of course, there is still a long way to go on the right-hand side, and you can see, even when both sides have been softened with a Pro Arte series F or Daler fan brush, there is still some coarseness of brush stroke, but I am content to keep this for the time being.

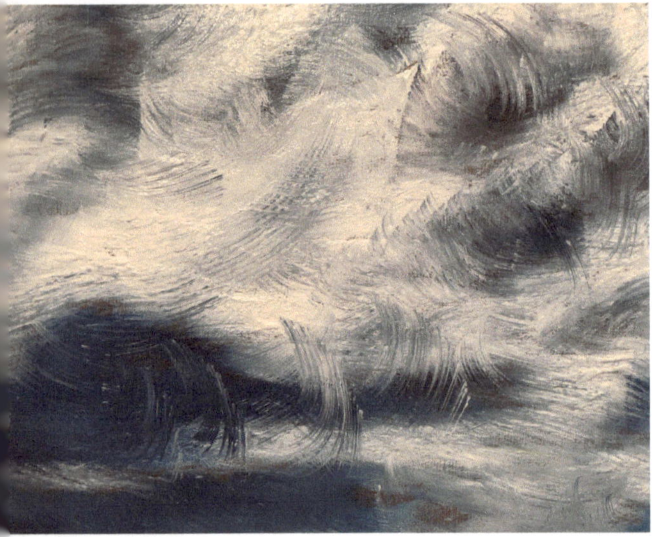

The swirling movement mimics the puff and billow of the clouds, so it helps to conveying movement and form.

To me, a sense of clouds bubbling over is being implied with that movement as it is uncontrolled and free.

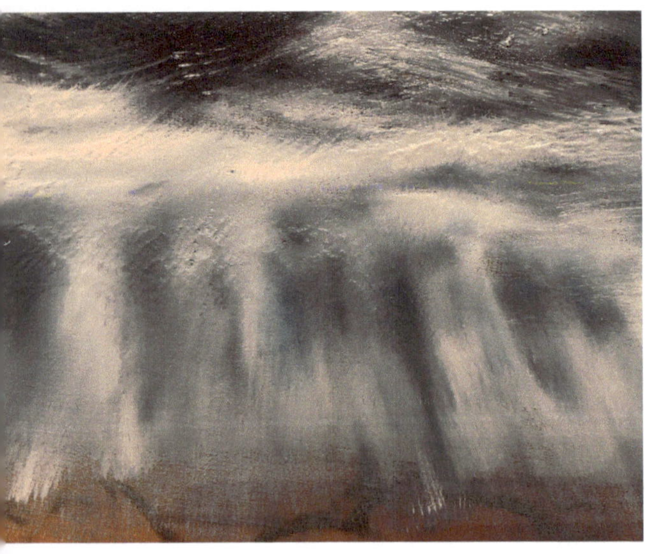

But now I want to tackle the underside of the clouds, just above where the light is spilling from them towards the horizon.

Using my Silverline Fan brush, I soften the downward strokes. To do this, I don't just follow the line of the brush stroke or the light. I take the brush from side to side too – in all directions – ensuring all edges blur.

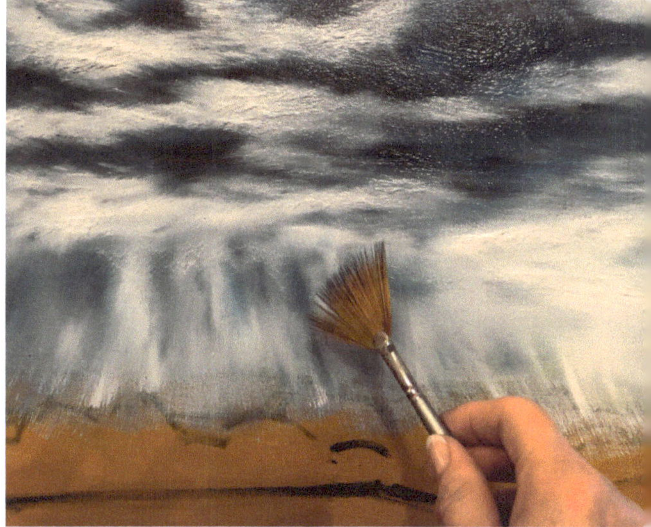

You may have to clean your brush on clean kitchen roll or tissue several times when doing this – or change brushes. I generally have at least three similar brushes in use at any one time when doing this, swapping between them as they become paint-laden. You will need to clean your brushes fully in between uses like this too, hence the reason why having several brushes to switch between works best.

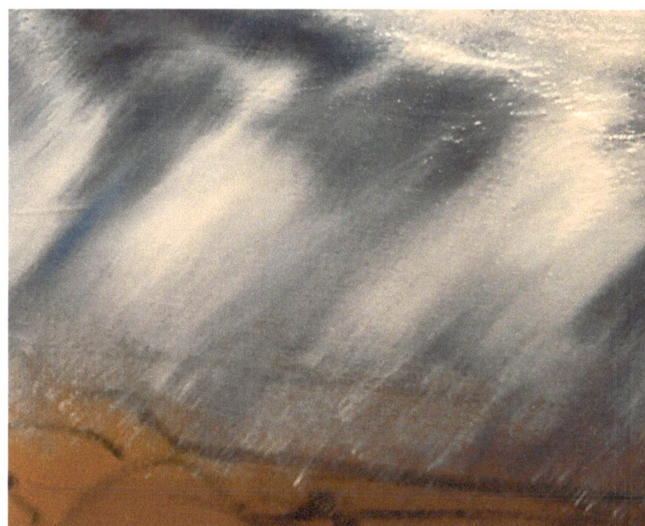

And here is the lower sky fully blended, and the sun being added. It is necessary to leave the canvas to dry a little once you start working on areas that you do not want contaminated by other colours, so this is a day later.

Notice I have, in the meantime, also softened up those coarser brushstrokes in the sky so the movement is still in the bubbling clouds, but it is now more implied than obvious.

The sun is a mix of white heat and yellow heat, so centre the white heat first and build up the more yellow sunshine around it, softening and blending as you go.

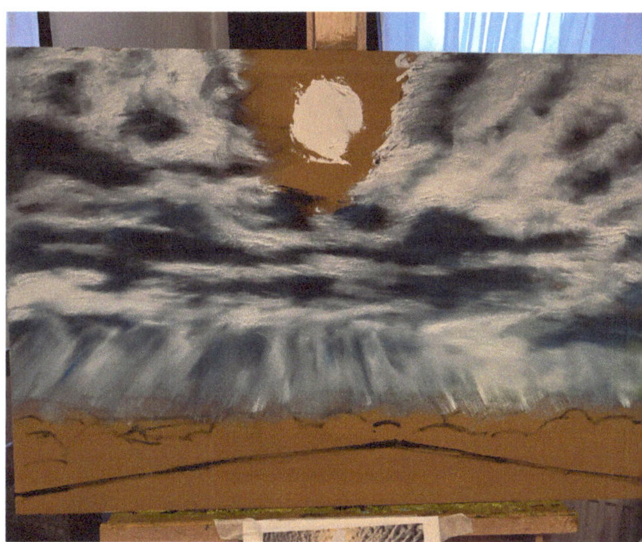

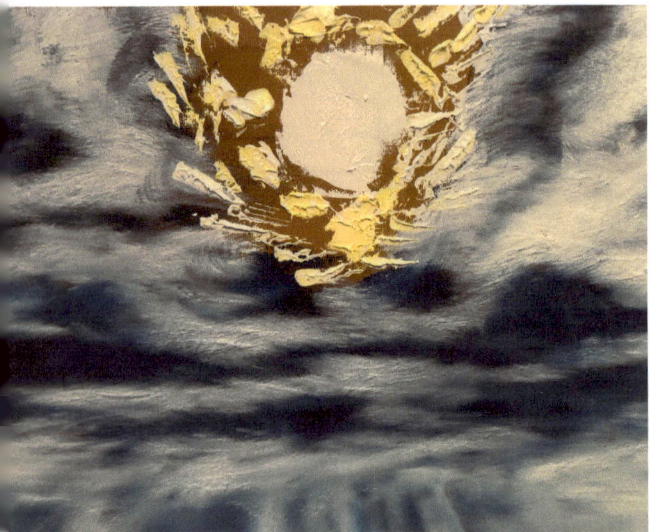
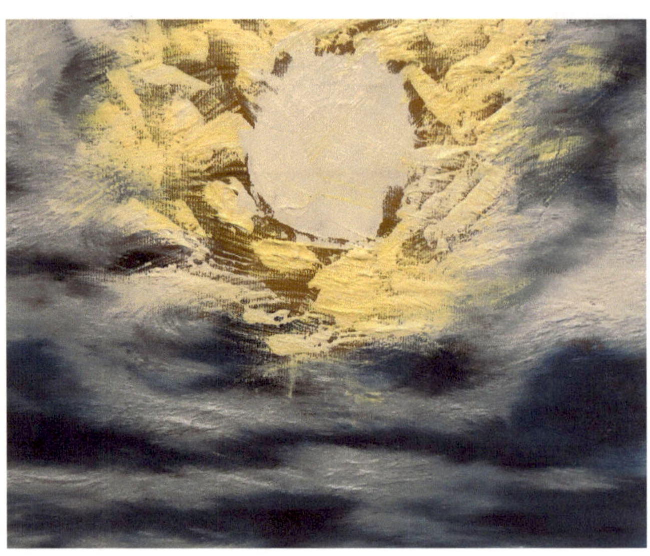

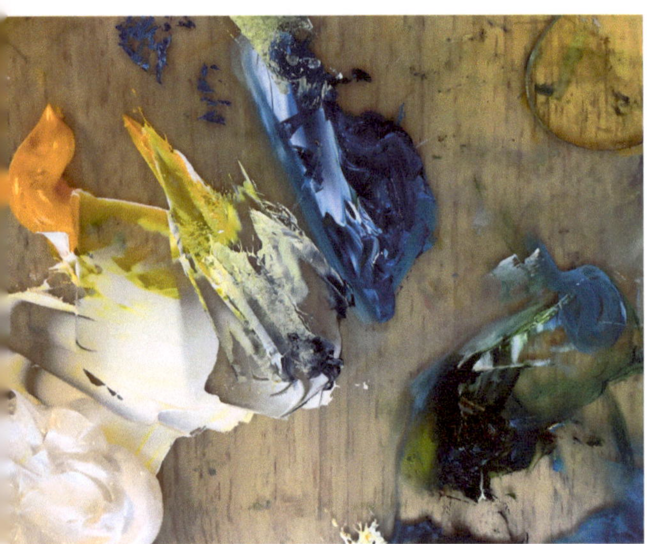

My palette here is based around Titanium White and Cadmium Yellow Deep.

I particularly like Cadmium Yellow Deep as it is such a warm colour, not acid as Lemon Yellow can be, and not as earthy as Yellow Ochre. It also has a deeper, richer texture and hue to Cadmium Yellow itself, which again, sometimes I find somewhat 'sharp'.

Continue blending, until you have a base, then you will need to use a palette knife to layer on sufficient pigment for the white areas to retain their opaqueness without colour contamination from the blue-sky pigment or the yellow sunlight drops.

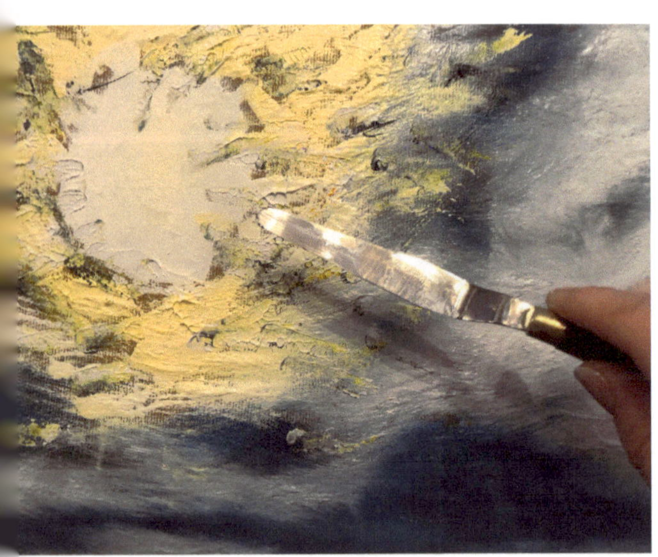
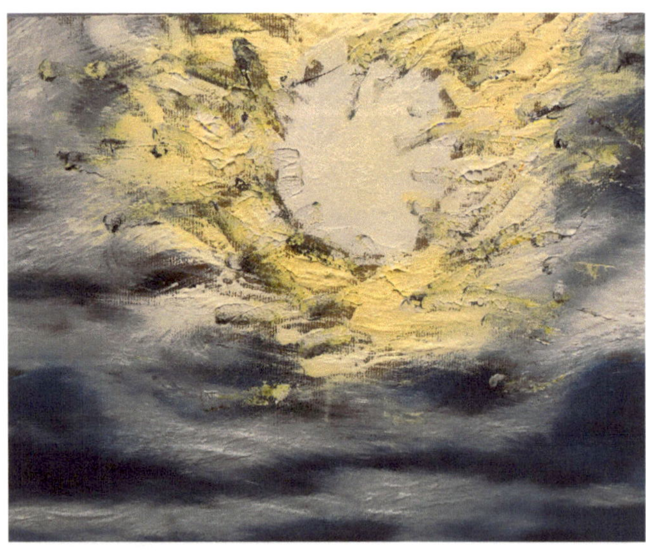

You will have to touch up several times during the blending process, until you are content with the depth of colour in the white centre but have sufficiently softened the rays of sunlight coming from the centre too.

Remember to clean your brush regularly or change brushes. When you get a build-up of paint on the brush, you won't be able to avoid transferring it – often in little spiky brush strokes – to a new area and then it will take a fair degree of remedial work to blend it out or cover it up!

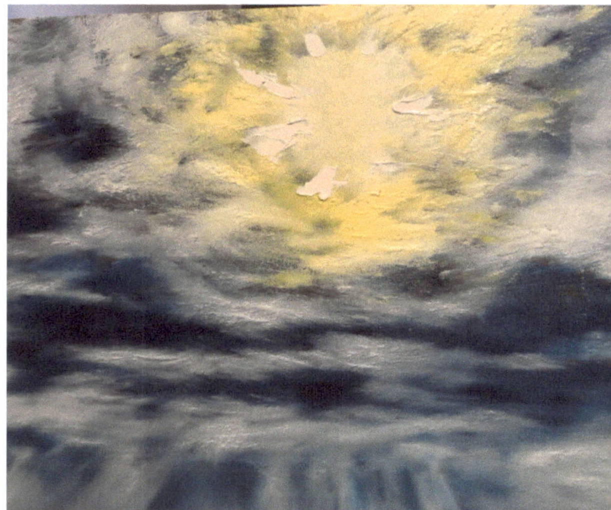

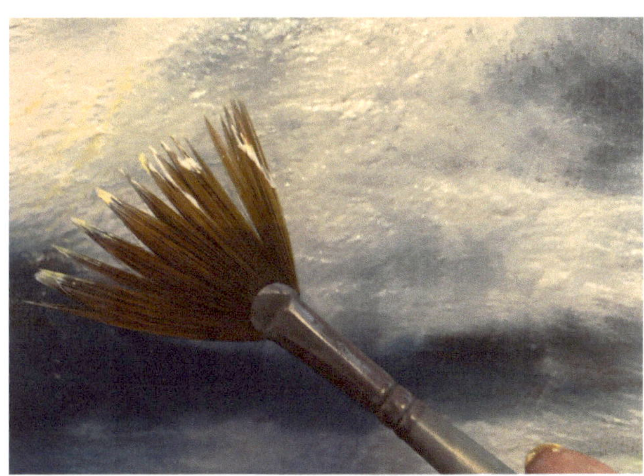

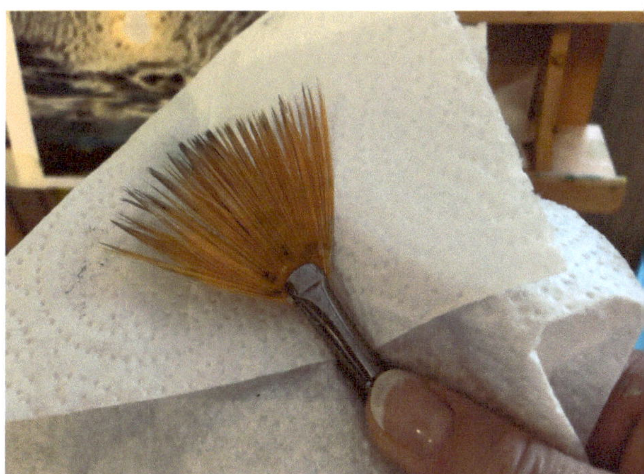

Once this stage is complete, stand back and survey the overall painting. Do you have enough highlights and lowlights? This point is always a good time to reflect on whether your painting is showing 'life' as well.

Sometimes, if it isn't. it's a simple as adding a few extra touches – as I did here…

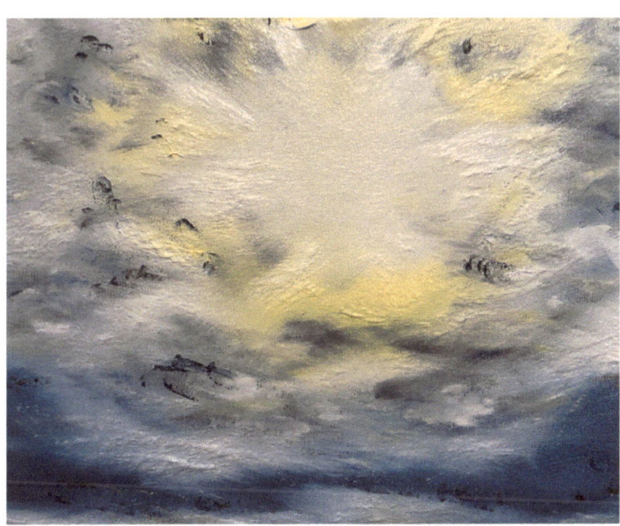

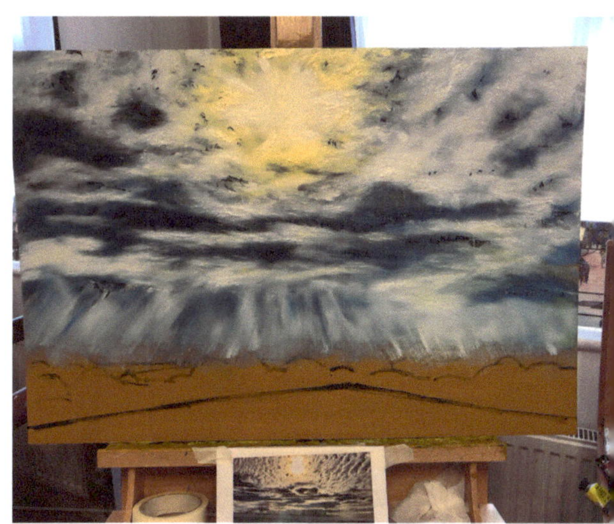

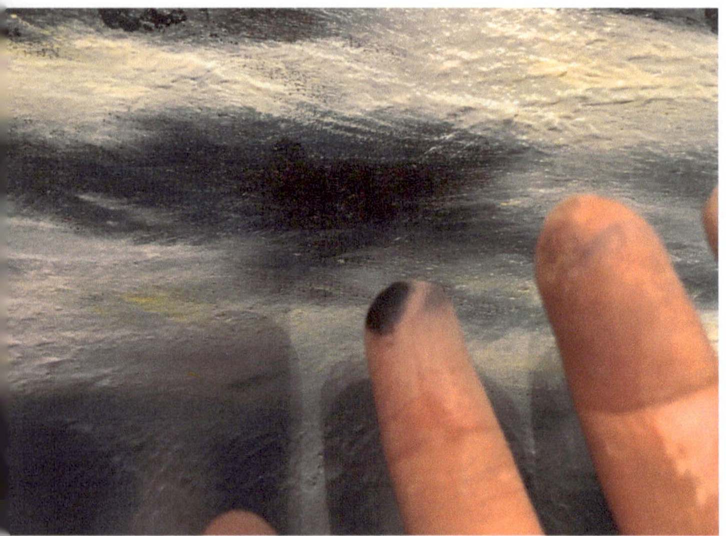

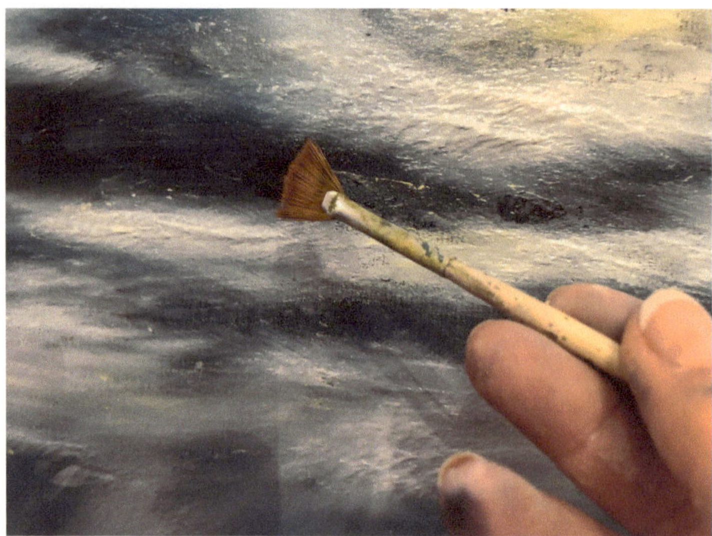

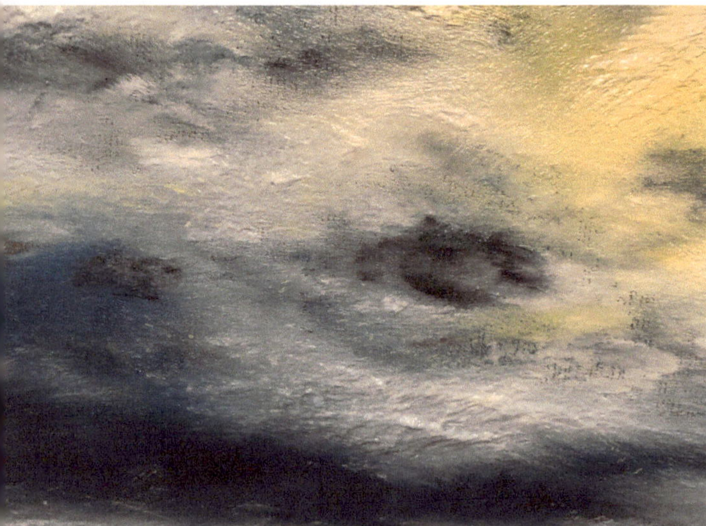

And if your fan brushes don't do the job perfectly in easing those lowlights into the rest of the painting, have you tried your fingers recently? Sometimes they are simply the only thing for the job …

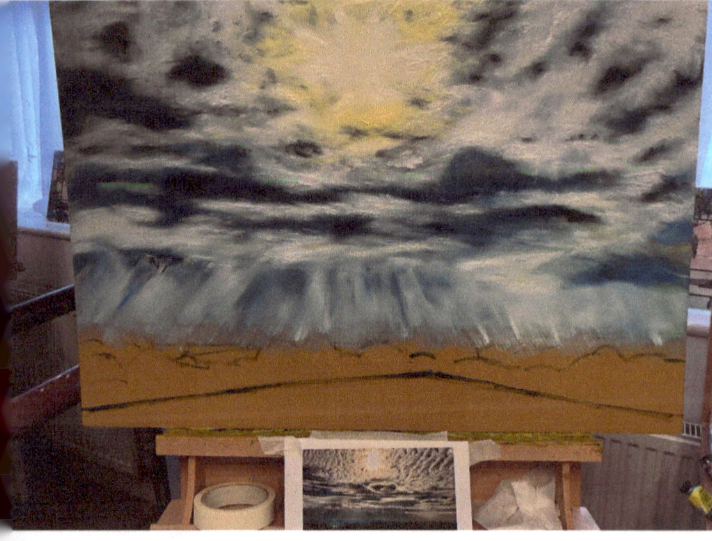

And that concludes the sky …

Apart from defining the horizon…

Which I will do by running a thin fan brush loaded with white paint along its edge and then soften it with another, clean, fan brush so that there isn't a sharp divide between horizon, land and sky, but there is a delineation.

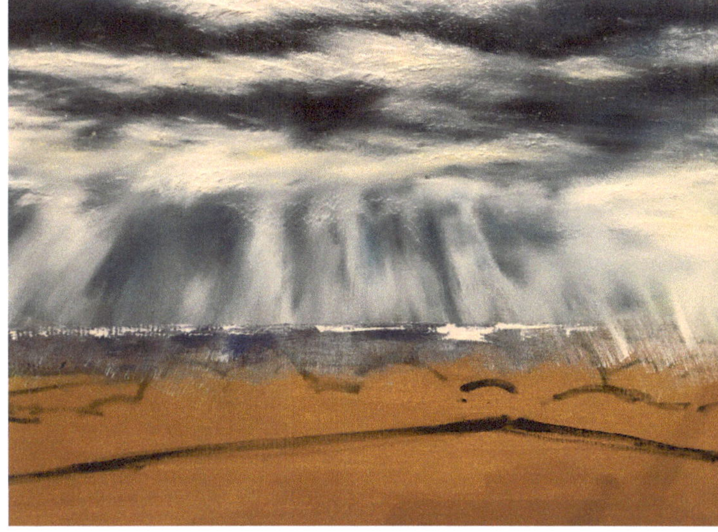

I use both upwards, downwards and sideways strokes for this.

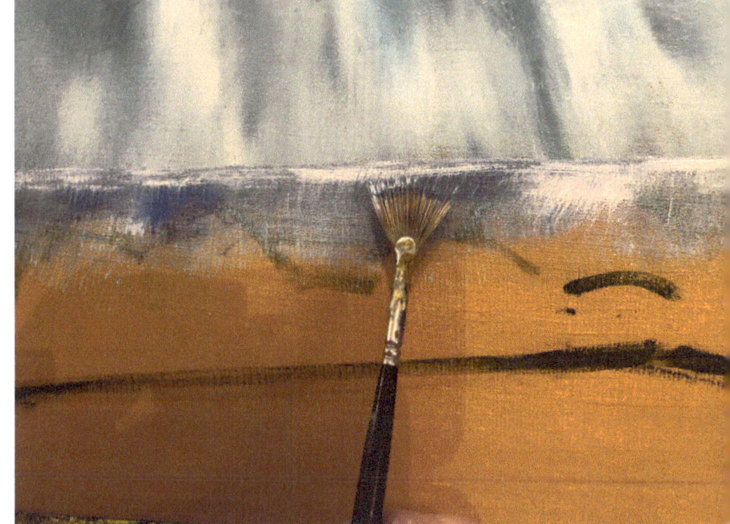

Patience is a virtue, they say, and the most wonderful thing about oil painting is that mistakes can be corrected long after they've been made. Either rub or scrape off still-wet paint or scrape it off if already dry or partially dry, or simply paint over it. However, the wise oil painter knows when to leave what they've done and wait … and this is exactly what you should do before progressing onto the land.

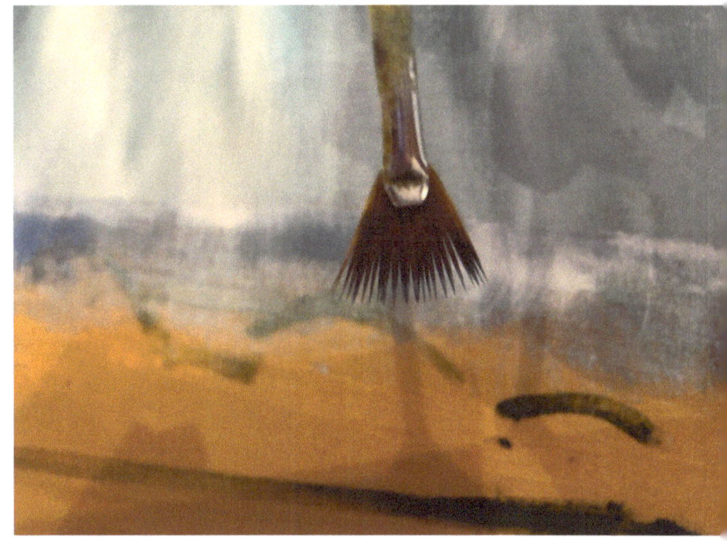

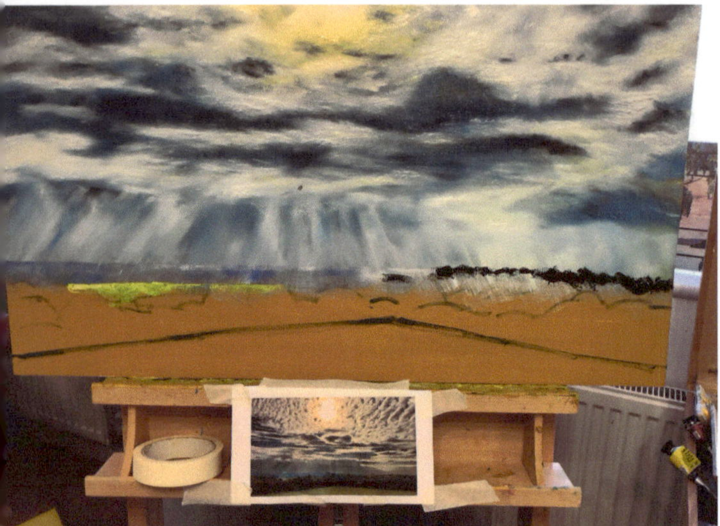

With the horizon suggested, and the painting of the sky starting to dry, now I can start work on the land below.

I start by blocking in the land – an under-colour green as I will be adding detail over the top of this.

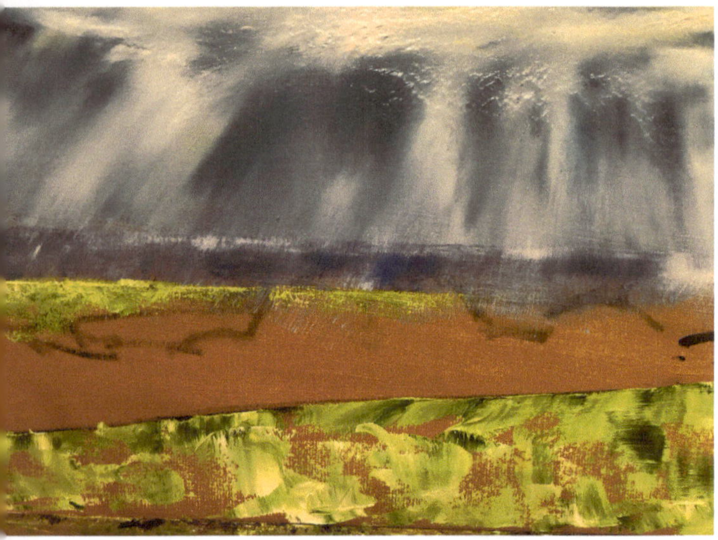

Once again, I need to pay attention to the horizon as the land coverage progresses and I usually find a palette knife edge gives a good sharp edge that can later be softened.

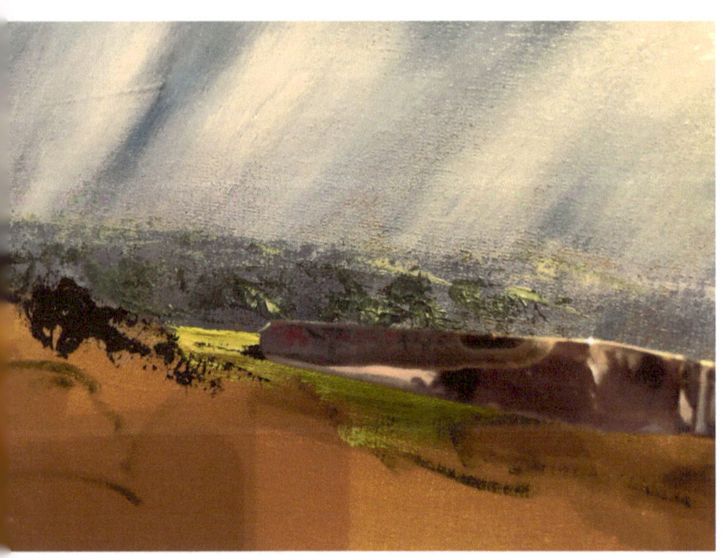

Using a palette knife is also a lot steadier and certain than using a fine paintbrush because you already have the straight edge of the palette knife to help. With a paintbrush, you must have a *very* steady hand.

You needn't worry about the line/edge left being overly-harsh because it can be softened later.

I am using the Silverline brush to do that here, but the extent of the softening will depend on what you are painting. For some edges, you do need a well-defined horizon or mountain edge, so experiment.

When I was first learning to oil paint – as with watercolours too – I had some 'experimental' boards. They suffered all kinds of mistreatment from me, but by doing that I learnt which effect was achieved by which piece of equipment, and the handling of it. Totally invaluable!

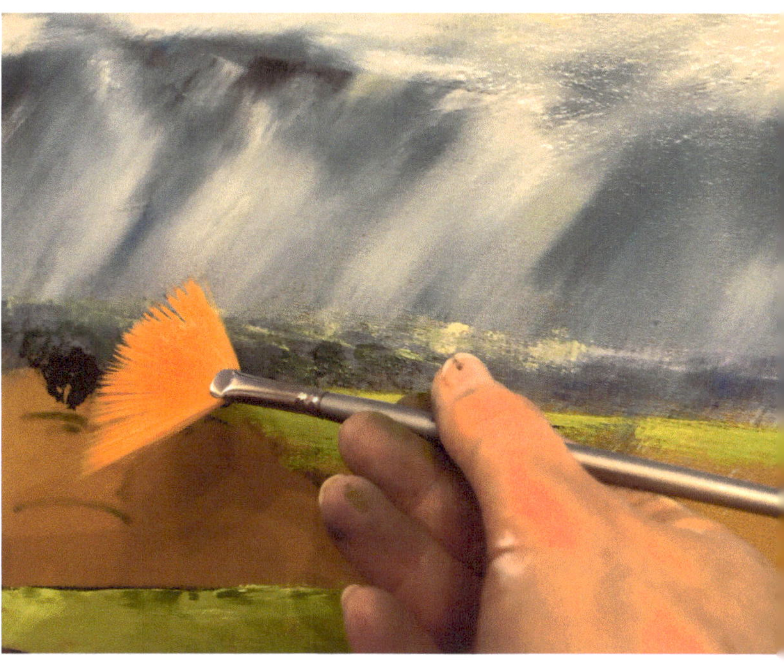

In this painting, you can see there is some defined horizon, but there will be a great deal of treeline too, so I have etched in what I need and then moved onto the treeline. And the treeline is varied – in both form and colour. Again, a lesson in colours – going back to section 2. There is no one green, there are thousands – probably millions – although our eyes can't differentiate that many. We can differentiate a lot though, so look for the varying shades of greens that you find within tree shapes – sometimes quite surprising.

My base colours here are Sap Green, Payne's Grey, Rose Tint, Cadmium Yellow Deep and Burnt Umber, and a touch of Titanium White. You notice a theme here with my choice of paints? Yes, I could probably paint nearly all my paintings with just those colours. Try it – using a limited palette is not only a test of your ingenuity in producing different hues, it also starts to build up a theme in your work as a painter. That's also why I always use Yellow Ochre for my under-painting.

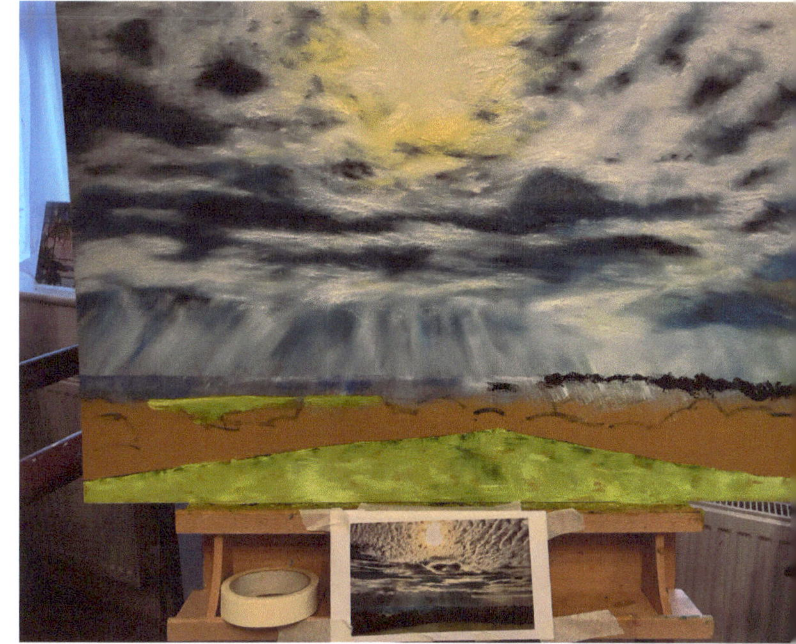

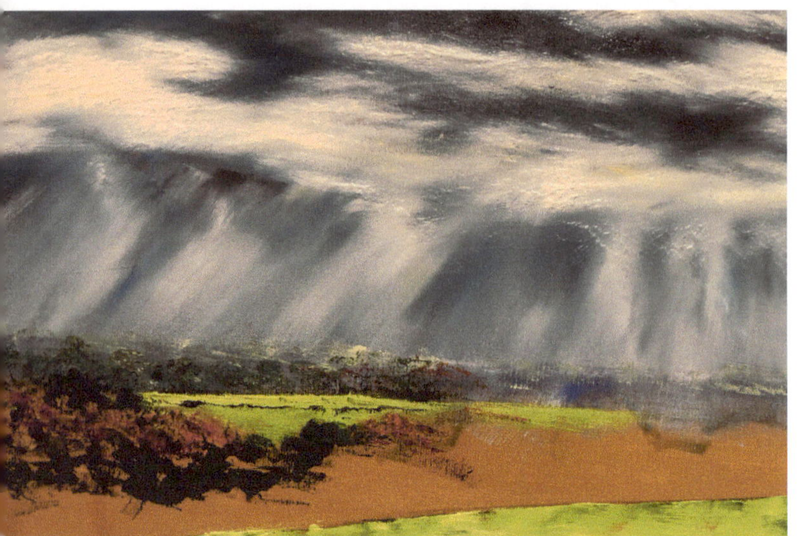

I rather like these particular greens and autumnal shades I have created from my limited palette though. They are warm and soothing, whereas the sky is tumultuous…

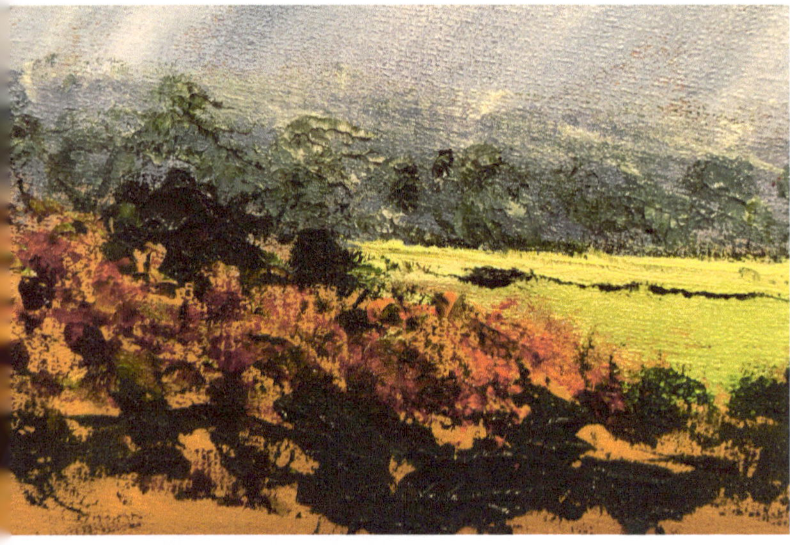

It is very powerful to establish complementary – but also sometimes jarring – tones in a painting. It will lend it a sense of the dramatic or the serene, depending on how you use them. Red-green? Clashes we say, but does it? No, they are opposites on the spectrum and if you build up to using a full colour wheel, you will see how used together judicially they can be both harmonious and extremely appealing too.

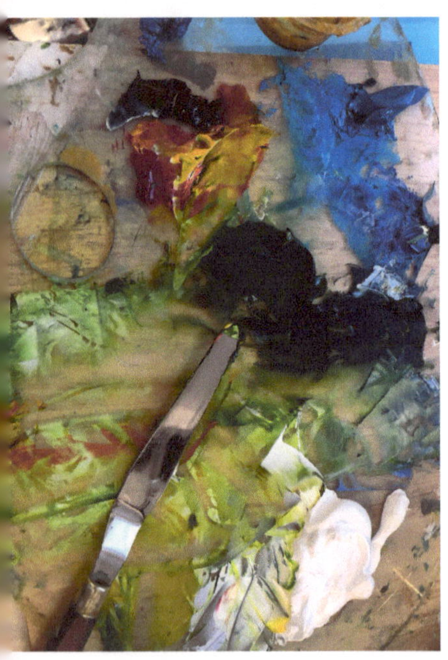

Here's my palete mid-mix: Cerulean Blue, French Ultramarine, Titanium White, Rose Tint, Umber, Payne's Grey and Sap Green. That's all I need for all those colours …

And then back to my trusty palette knife to apply edges and blocked-in colour.

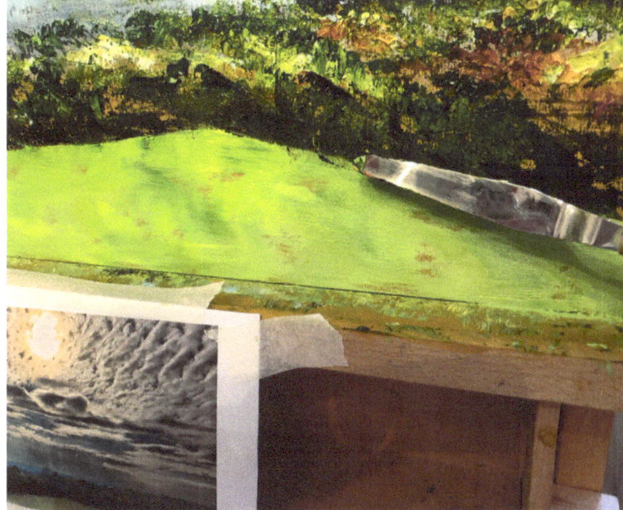

Some stippling with a bristle fan brush to deeepen shadows or identify highlights …

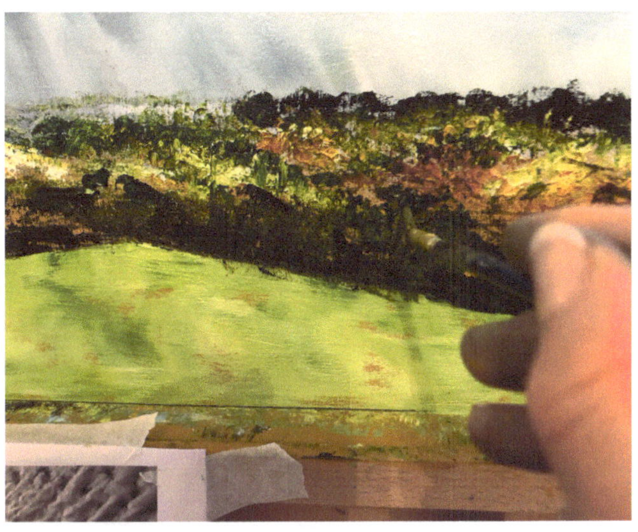

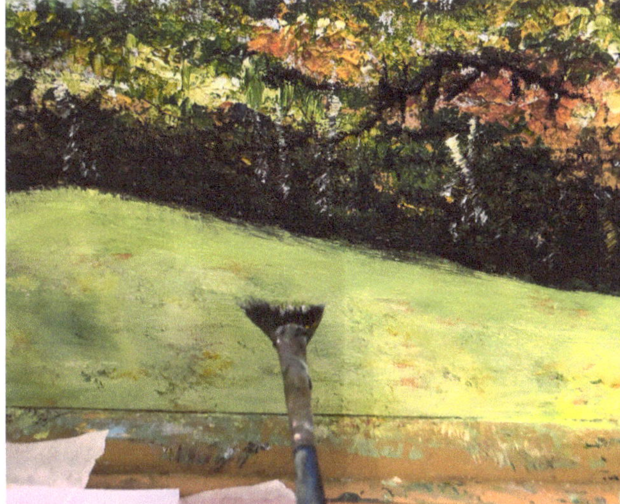

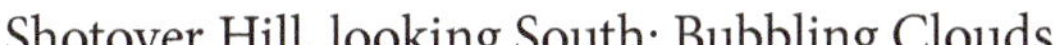

And I'm done.

Shotover Hill, looking South: Bubbling Clouds.

I can't leave skies and clouds this incredible without a few words – or maybe more than a few – about how this kind of image sparks my imagination in so many other ways. Here's one of them: a snippet of a story I am working on currently about a man having his life turned upside down, whilst sitting in the middle of a field and gazing into the distance. This extract is from a short way in, just after he's found out he made a pact with the devil, many, many years ago, and it's about to run out. Very fitting to be sitting under bubbling skies for that situation, I think! I hope you enjoy the little bit of intrigue and the skies that inspired it. The extract may someday become 'Those about to Die'…

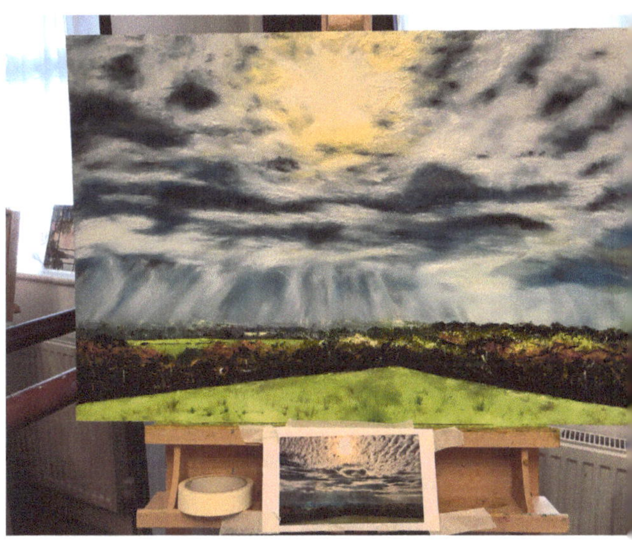

"'You take my soul?'

He burst out laughing again – the same whimsical good humour that had accompanied his reply to my sarcastic enquiry about the number of times that he'd died reappeared.

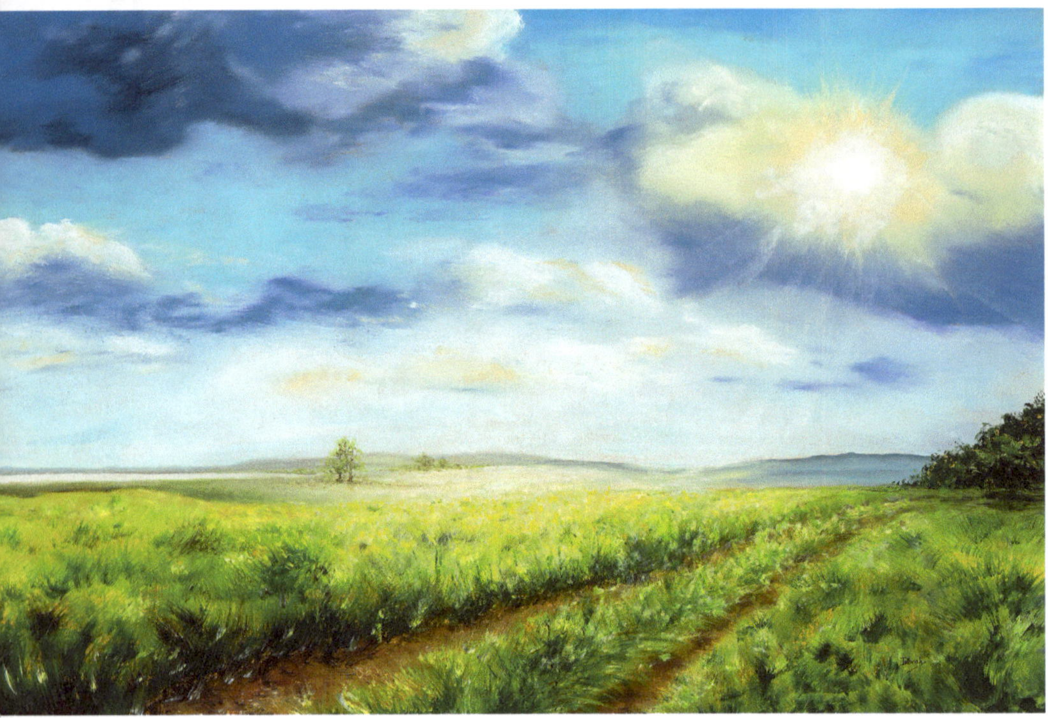

'Your face – you should see it,' he gasped between bouts of hilarity. I was about to respond, witheringly, but words suddenly failed me. Behind the twinkling eyes and good-natured grin, there was something else that made my blood run cold.

I shook my head shakily. The serenity of the rolling hills and sunlit clouds has left me.

'That's impossible. All of what you're saying is impossible. You don't exist, this conversation never happened and I'm not sitting on a wall in the middle of nowhere discussing rubbish with a madman.'

He climbed slowly back up the bank and heaved himself onto the wall beside me again.

'No.' He swept his arm out on a wide gesture, encompassing the landscape as if it belonged solely to him and he was giving it to me. 'You're not sitting on a wall in the middle of nowhere discussing nonsense with a non-existent madman.' I followed the sweep of his arm and the green of the grass slowly disintegrated before my eyes, morphing effortlessly into another colour; blue – deep, deep blue. Blue, as far as the eye could see, filling every crack and crevasse of my being with its intensity, broken only spasmodically by the tiniest puff of cloud, bubbling – *bubbling*! I gasped, gazing from mid-heaven back down to lower earth. Around me the sky billowed with popping scabs of blue-grey cirrus, their crisping rims illuminated by incandescent yellow spotlights of sunshine. I winced at their fluorescence, turning my gaze downwards, despite the reluctance to because far below us the tiny dots of a toy town and its toy people swarmed and scattered. The jib arm of the crane we were sitting on, hundreds of feet above the toy town, lurched and trembled as a gust of wind sent it swinging further into the blue. If it had been a roller coaster ride it would have been spectacular. My head swam and my heart clenched into a knot. I gasped in the rarefied atmosphere of the world of immortality and contracts bartering years more of life in return for souls that apparently existed far above the earth.

'Jesus, H Christ!' I squeezed my eyes shut and clutched desperately at the unforgiving steel of the crane. The burn of bile rose in my throat and forced tears from the corners of my lids. All around me the sky turned to Armageddon, and me in it's throes.

'No blaspheming, *please.*' I could hear the amusement in his voice, but I didn't care. I was going to die. DIE… 'And do open your eyes and enjoy the view whilst you can. Life is all about knowledge and experience, after all – isn't that what you told me once?'

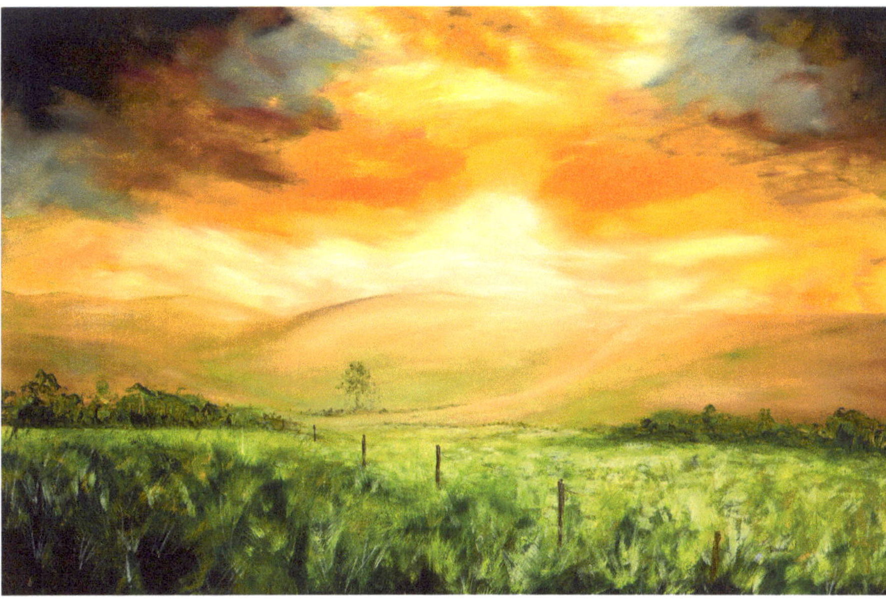

I counted the beats of my heart and wondered how it didn't explode, holding on tight just in case it didn't, and I made it back down to the ground in one piece instead of many. Then I opened my eyes, more out of the need for one last look at the world before I plummeted to a mess of splintered bone and split flesh than courage. The fresh green of the rolling valley sprawled in front of me once more, punctuated with poppies and Dutch Barns; the red of Armageddon became soothing normality.

'What the …'

He laughed, an explosion of humour.

'So why *are* we here?'

'I don't know! Why should I know?'

'Well, you asked me to meet you here, in this precise location. You said you were ready to jump. I assumed that meant you were ready to jump onto number thirty, early. It appears you aren't?' The question was accompanied by a raised eyebrow and a half smile.

'Suicide? I never asked you to help me kill myself. I don't want to die. This is crazy! I was walking down the road to the sandwich bar, thinking about whether to have egg mayo or chicken salad and … and … nothing! Wham – here I was, with you asking

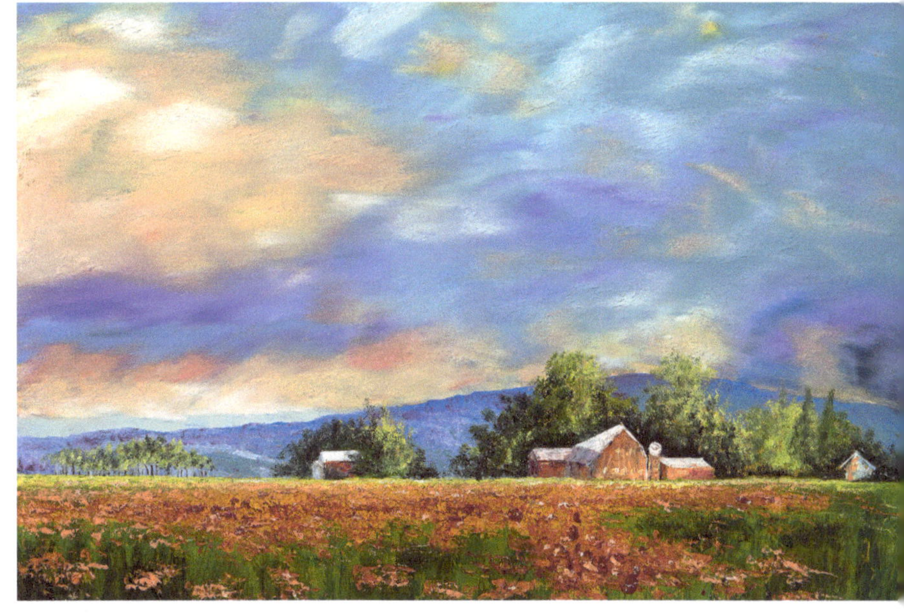

if it was time to move on. I have absolutely no intention of dying or of handing my soul over to anyone – least of all you!'

'So, why *are* we here?' he repeated. I wondered if his question was intended as the precursor to some profound but pointless discussion about the meaning of life or this really was just a dream. At another time and in another place, the discussion would have enthralled me, but not now. Even so, logic wanted to prevail. *Please let this be a dream*, I begged in my head. Let this be a dream where nonsensical incredibility is mixed with small elements of reality so that I can't quite dismiss it all as impossible. A dream born out of overactive imagination and … *Lena* …"

PART 4: GETTING STARTED
– TECHNIQUES

There are many ways to paint, this is just mine, and you should experiment until you find the way that suits you best, but here are a few ideas to start with:

Colour

A bit – or in fact, rather a lot – on colour…

Colour is the heart and soul of your painting. Of course, it is manipulated and blended, modified and texturised, but it is what creates how your viewer responds to an image in ways far more intriguing and compelling than you would first believe. We all see colour slightly differently. The human eye and the brain together translate light into colour. Indeed, the light sensitive retina is even considered to be a part of the brain. Light receptors within the eye transmit messages to the brain, and the brain then produces the familiar sensations of colour which it has compiled since birth. It was Isaac Newton who showed us that colour is not inherent in objects. Rather it is the surface of an object and how that surface reflects light that creates some colours and absorbs others, thus creating what we eventually perceive as its colour.

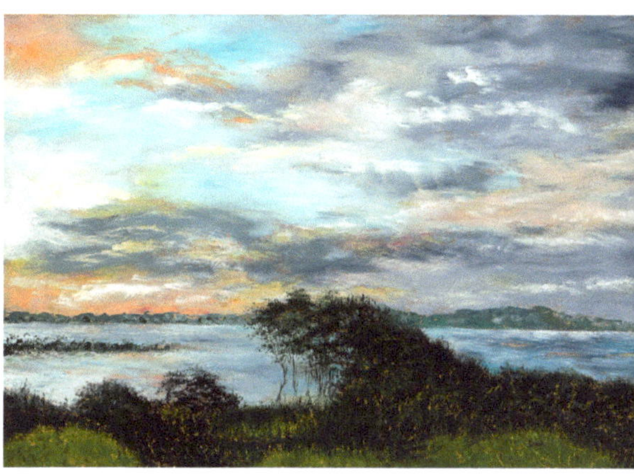

But colour has a role far more important than merely defining an object's specific properties of shape and hue. It is also what enables our remembrance of objects, influences our associations, and formulates our likes and dislikes. It even sparks our emotions…

Red stimulates and excites the brain – danger, red flags, fire …

Orange elicits feelings of excitement, warmth, and playfulness – sunsets, fruits, autumn shades …

Yellow draws attention and encourages positive emotions – sunlight, summer and so on.

Green is calming and cool – freshly mown grass, tree foliage, rolling hills …

Blue improves concentration – cool, deep water, distant misty mountains ... Sometimes it is also associated with sadness – 'the blues'; but even the blues are a very cerebral form of response to emotion.

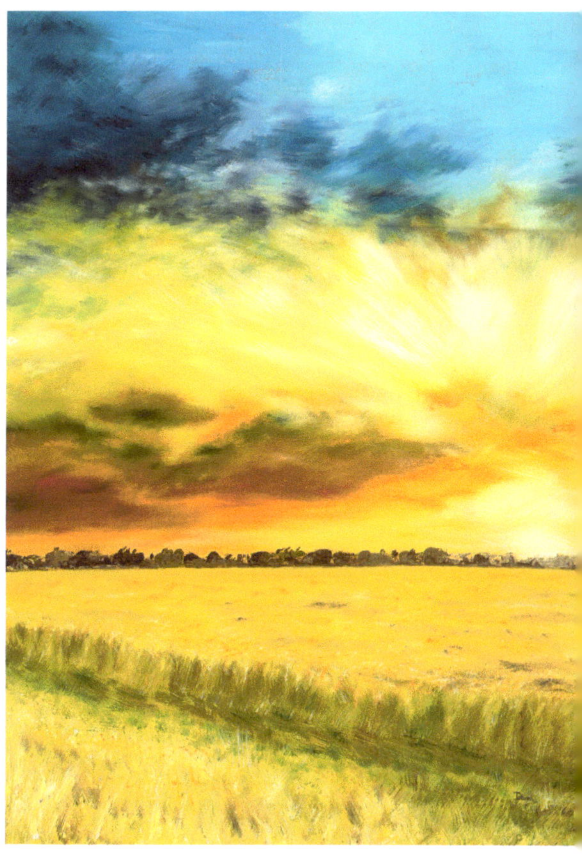

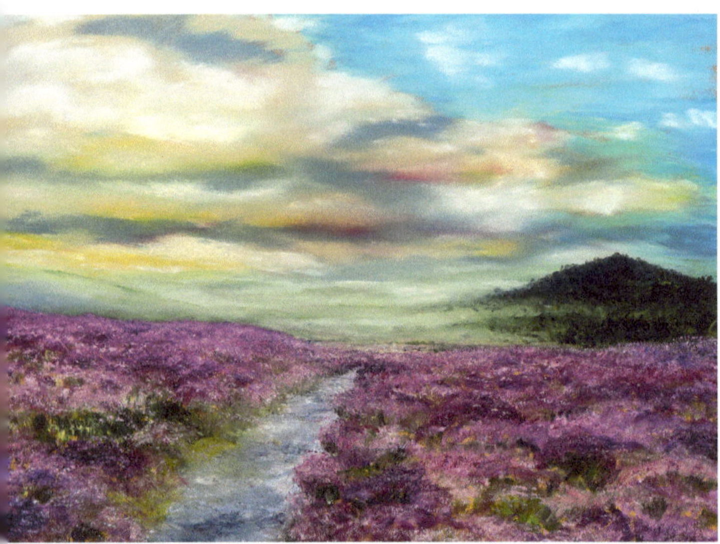

Purple is rich and royal and powerful; ermine robes, the solemnity of the processional – or the funereal …

Pink is all frothiness and femininity, but also associated with fun and health; 'tickled pink', 'in the pink' and so on …

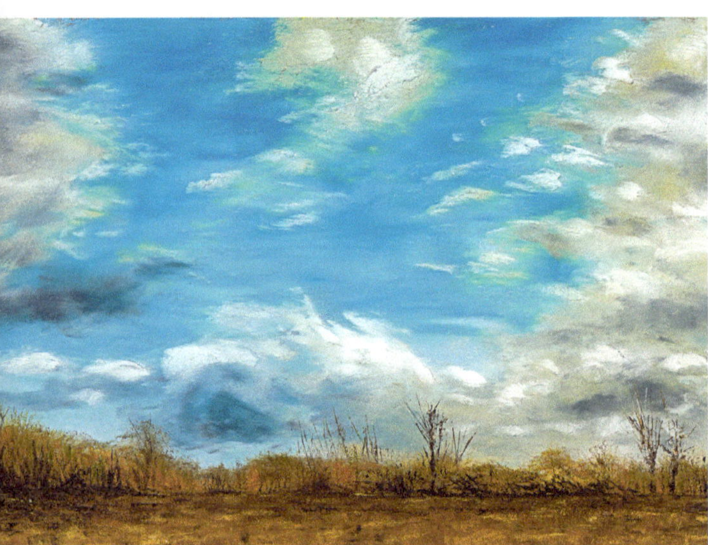

Brown is all earthiness and solidity, maybe mixed with the warmth of autumnal shades.

Black is sombre, serious and dark …

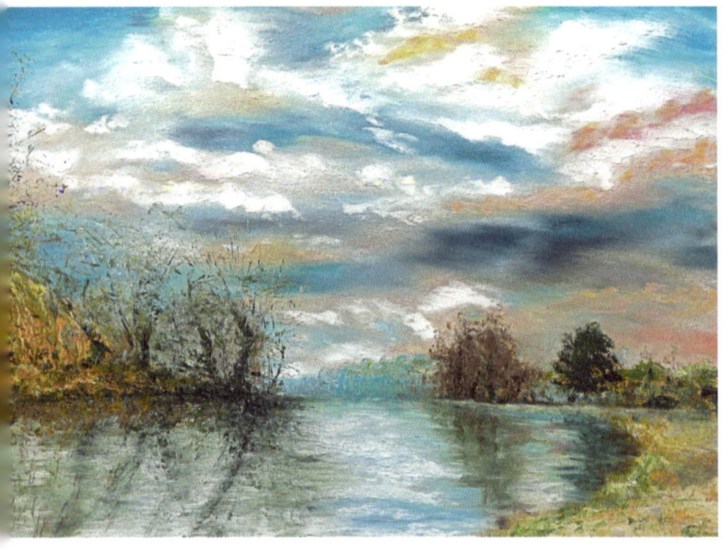

And cool white is associated with angels and purity, but also – contrarily – sterility; so white is a double-edged sword, but used judiciously it can also be peaceful and calming.

How do you see colours? I tried to define my understanding of them once by attaching them to people I love in this poem:

My family

I see my family in colours.
My older daughter is red, ruby red.
She flicks the crimson tip
of a wicked tongue across each lip.
Vamp, harlot, studious geek,
'call me 'Scarlet', she will cheek.
And yet sweet sixteen is as wholesome too
as a red summer apple that is crisp and new.

Deep purple, and moody;
my younger daughter -
inscrutable as China, mutable as water.
Like the pile on velvet, she's deep like a sigh,
silk to the touch when her spirits are high.
Yet suddenly abrasive, angrily contrary
when her adolescent nap is brushed the wrong way.

My yellow dog -
a golden blur
of tail and fur.
Lolling tongue – a smiley face;
smiles aren't just for the human race.
Stretched out like a long yellow rug,
'rub my tummy, give me a hug...'

Deep brown; the father that was.
Deep as the brown of the earth
the dust to dust, the dearth.
A warm autumn brown as the leaves' hues turn deeper,
not harvested by the seasons, but by the reaper.
Always steady under the feet of our past.
Man may die, but love will last.

And finally, me.
What colour do I see?
The colour blue; reflective, sad.
Surveying past and future; good and bad.
I've watched my family grow and evolve,
childhoods have passed, and death's forced its resolve.
Yet my life continues, ebbing blue, flowing true, like the sea.
I will look forward to the colours still to be.

But there is yet more … The visible spectrum for humans falls between ultraviolet and red light. Scientists estimate that humans can distinguish up to ten million colours, but we rarely realise that we see this vast number. We tend to allocate them merely to the basics; to red or blue or green. Why? The retina has two different types of cells that detect and respond to light; rods and cones. These cells are called photoreceptors. Rods are activated in low light, cones in bright light. We have roughly 6 million cones, and 110 million rods. Cones contain photo pigments, of which there are three types; red, green and blue. You see?

There is a lot more to seeing colour than this, but as this isn't a treatise on how we see colour but how we present it and then what we do with that presentation, I'm going to focus on what we can do with colour when we *really* paint with it.

Past visual experiences with objects always influence our perception of colour. This is referred to as colour constancy. Colour constancy ensures that the perceived colour of an object stays much the same when seen in different conditions, even though rods and cones will present the colour either as a specific colour or as grey-scale, depending on light conditions. For example, if you looked at a lemon under a red light, you would still think the lemon is yellow, even though you are now seeing in grey scale because the rods are active, not the cones.

But here's when you can bend the rules, because now you know you *perceive* colour, not that colour *IS*, you can take all that you now know about colour and how you record it, and use it to record and present images in the way you want them perceived by your viewers. Are sunsets really this colour? Or is it just how we remember them? Both probably.

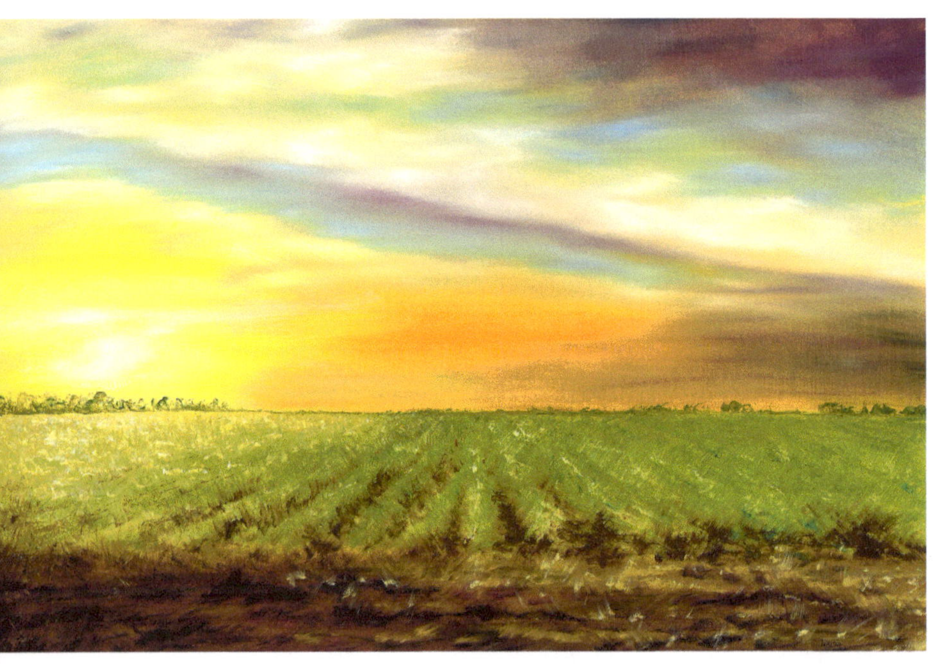

Use colour to emote as well as represent. For me, sunsets and dawn sunrises are the most glorious of visuals; bursts of red and gold and peachy-pink that inspire me to start a new day or reflect on what has happened in one just ending. Thus, they tell a visual story, and an actual one too. If you can use colour to present your own visual story, you are well on the way to mastering paint and its ability to influence your onlooker in a way as powerful as any personal experience can.

That's why I enjoyed painting this sunset so much:

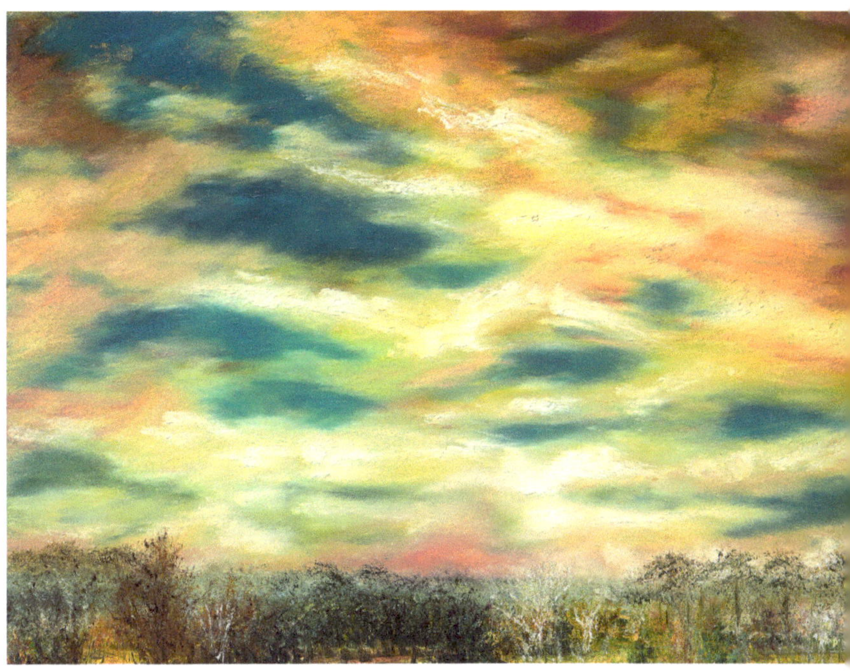

The first person I showed it to (my wonderful partner, as it happens) exclaimed, 'Wow! Looks like the second coming!' Now that's what I like to hear – an emotive (and cultural) reaction as well as a visual one…

Having said all of that, it's important to get to know your colours too. As previously mentioned, I often work with a limited palette yet the colours I create from it are amazingly vibrant and varied.

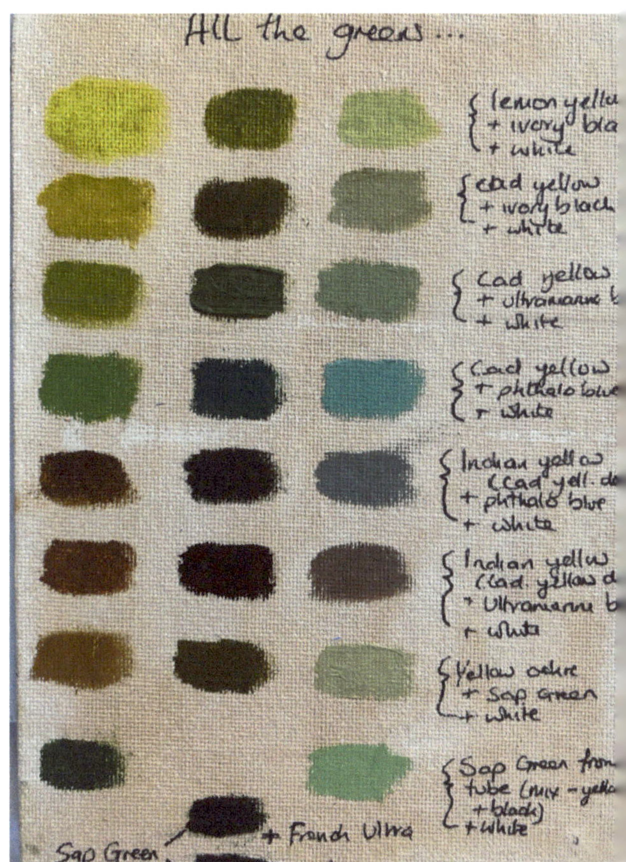

A good exercise to get to know your colours and your palette is to take a specific colour and add others to it, recording what you achieve from the mix, like this example of working with greens – one of my favourite colours.

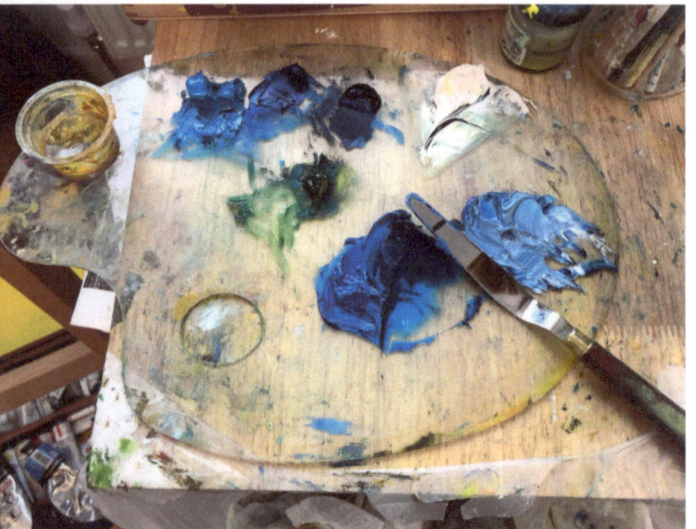

Whilst the perceived advice is to clean up your palette regularly, and only work on specific blocks/ tints of one colour at a time, I am not an exponent of that. I find I work best with a range of colours in use simultaneously. In my way of using colour synergistically, it flows together as I work with it and automatically creates depth and form as such. Often that also includes applying paint not in specific blocks, but in ranges. For example, on this working palette you will see the colours flowing into each other even as I add them to the board.

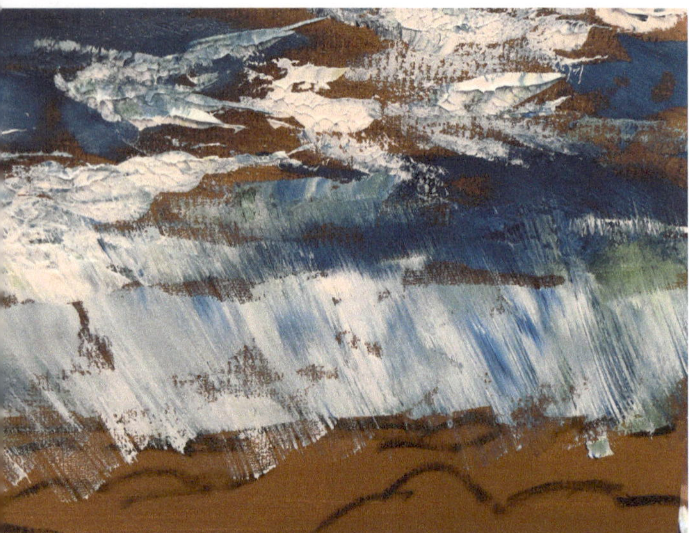

And in this painting, you see how that works in practice on the board itself …

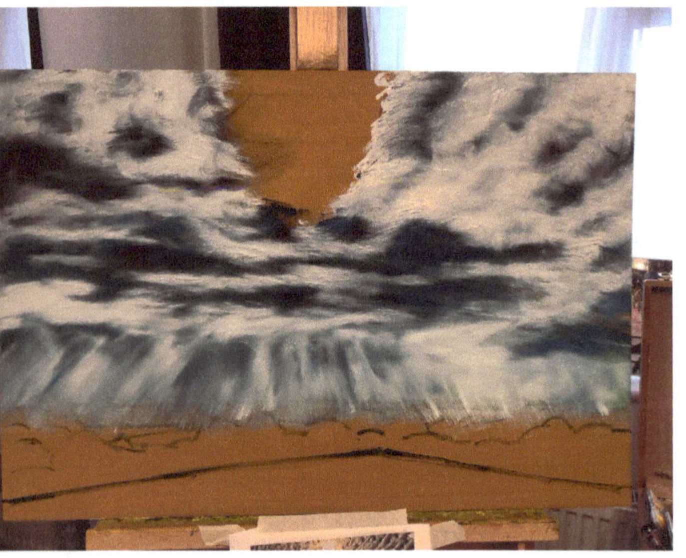

…and then after being smoothed to create the downward light effect from the clouds cast by the sunlight breaking through.

The story of this painting is covered step by step in Part 3: Skies.

For a basic sky painting:

Use:
Titanium White
Ultramarine Blue or Cerulean Blue (I love Cerulean but sometimes a mix of FU and CB is good).
Payne's Grey
Burnt Umber – sometimes.

For a cold, crisp blue sky, under-paint with French Ultramarine and Liquin. For a warm blue sky, under-paint with Yellow Ochre and Liquin (my favourite).

You can sketch in the outline of the white clouds if you feel happier doing this, or you can block in the blue-sky areas around where the clouds are without sketching them in.

Paint in the white clouds, blending and smoothing them with a fan brush to soften the edges but keeping the tops crisp/defined unless you want more wispy cloud formations. Add Payne's Grey on top of the wet white, but near the base of the cloud area, and blend in to create their shadow area. Generally, leave a thin white rim area to define the base of the clouds.

Wispy clouds can also be created within the blue-sky area by using your fingers, or with small taps of the palette knife or a scratchy brush to leave feathery trails that can then be smoothed over later.

Other skies:

For yellowish stormy skies use Titanium White, Payne's Grey, Yellow Ochre, Cadmium Yellow, Burnt Umber.

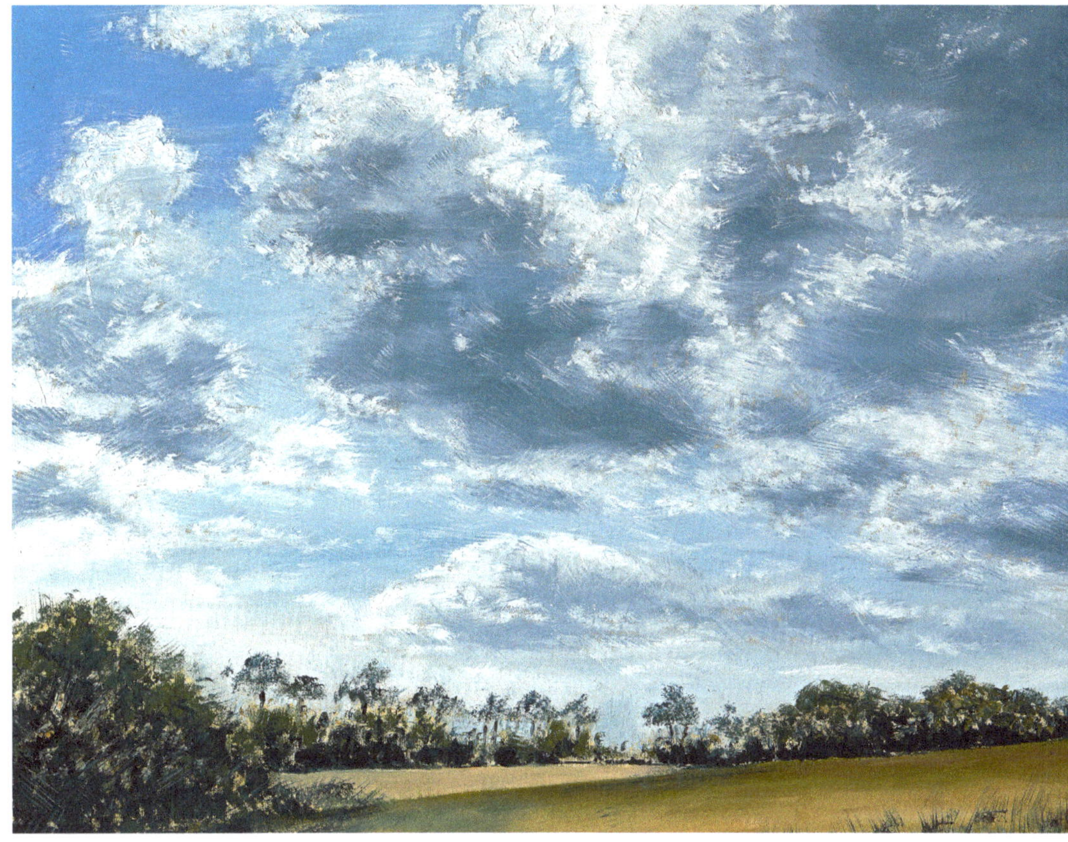

For mauve-ish stormy skies use Titanium White, Ultramarine Blue (or Cerulean for a more Mediterranean hue), Burnt Umber, Alizarin Crimson. You can also use – sparingly – Permanent Mauve.

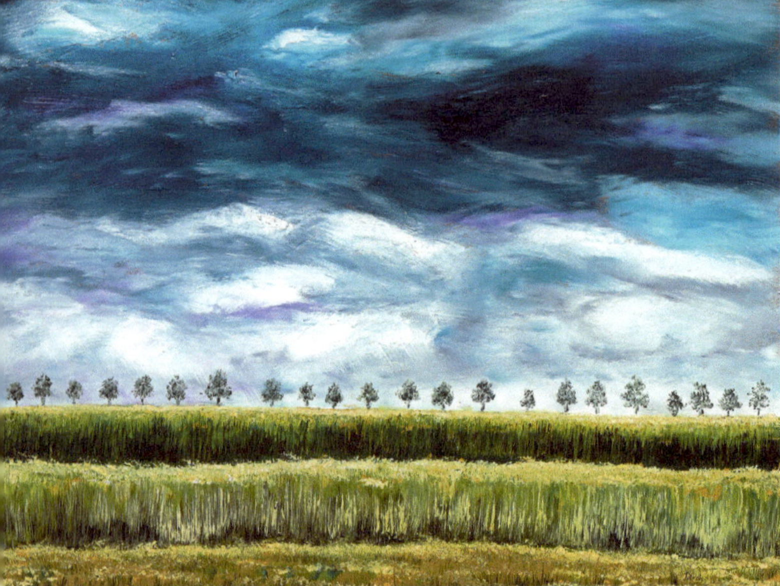

For dawns and sunsets use Titanium White, Ultramarine Blue (or Cerulean for a more Mediterranean hue), Burnt Umber, Alizarin Crimson, Permanent Rose.
Be careful not to end up 'chocolate-boxy'.

Some specifics about clouds:
- The sky is lighter on the edge of the horizon.
- The position of the sun will define/dictate the dark areas in clouds.
- Clouds are larger overhead at the top of the canvas/board and look smaller/ more numerous at eye level and on the far horizon.
- There is often more than one type of cloud in the sky, depending on temperature, atmospheric pressure, wind, humidity and likely precipitation (rain). Get to know your cloud formation types.
- Sometimes clouds and colours can look unreal, but remember the truth is often stranger than fiction. This is a sunset sky looking out from my front door in mid-January.
- Sunsets can be very difficult as they perform best with the more expensive paints, especially transparent oils – although I haven't used any transparent oils in the paintings in this book. However, be careful of lightening colours with too much white as it can make the colour look opaque.
- Think about the composition of the painting, and the tonal areas. Try to make them harmonious with the composition of the painting overall, even if you have to be a little creative with them.
- Remember the one third, two thirds division

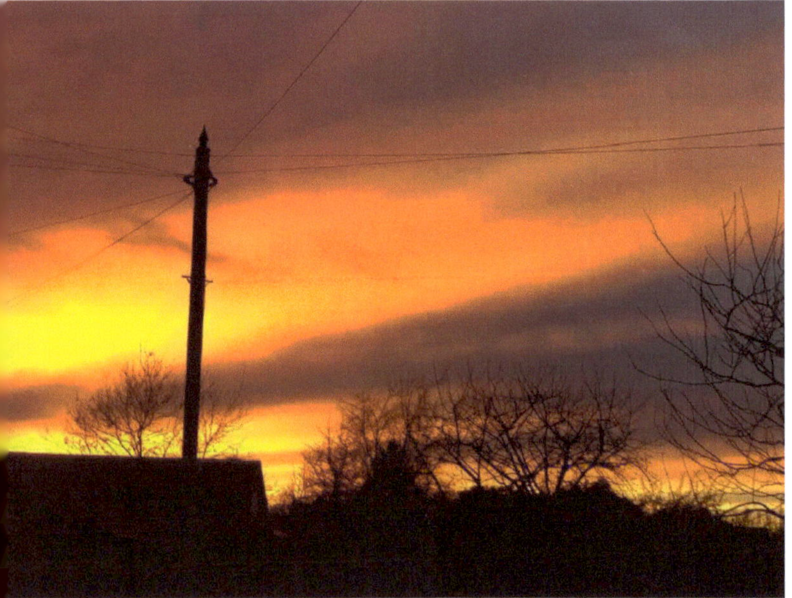

rule: *one-third* land and *two-thirds* sky, about a quarter of the way up the canvas – see below under composition.

Trees and landscapes:

Great greens start here:
Titanium White
Lemon Yellow
Cadmium (or Chrome) Yellow
Ultramarine Blue
Cerulean Blue
Yellow Ochre
Burnt Umber
Possibly – Ivory Black – as it's earthier than Payne's Grey

Under-paint with Yellow Ochre, diluted with Liquin for a warm landscape, or Ultramarine Blue for a winter scene – although I tend to add some warmth to all my paintings by opting for Yellow Ochre as standard.

Winter trees – bare branches – are best painted over a dried background with a fine round sable brush or etched in with a palette knife edge. It's all about painting in pattern and structure. Study the shape of the tree thoroughly first, including making some precursory sketches if necessary.

Verdant trees are best painted in a number of stages, bearing in mind the greens of the other foliage and landscape around them. Treat them as tonal shapes, ignoring the detail, until they are all blocked into the composition, but don't fall into the trap of thinking bark is brown and leaves are green. They are often grey-green/sand-coloured, and even black, depending on shadows and lighting.

1. Draw in the tree structure.
2. Using two main tones of your chosen green, paint in the two main tonal areas of light and dark.
3. Now add further shades of green to highlight.
4. Leave the 'sky holes' – the areas where the sky shows through branches – unpainted. Sky holes are generally slightly darker than the surrounding area of sky otherwise they will pop out at you because they are being juxtaposed against the darker green.
5. Distant trees are always lighter and fainter.
6. Remember that 'less is more' when painting in foliage, which I usually stipple in with a bristle fan brush or a stipple brush.

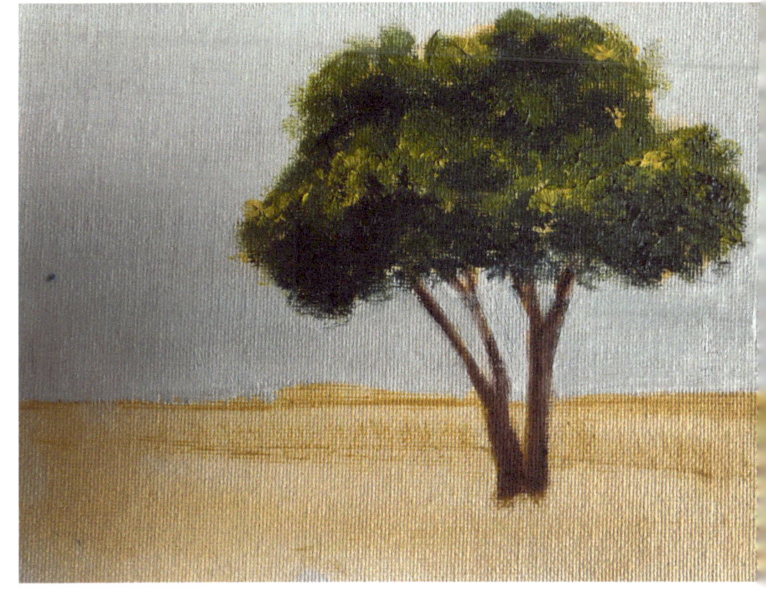

Form and composition:

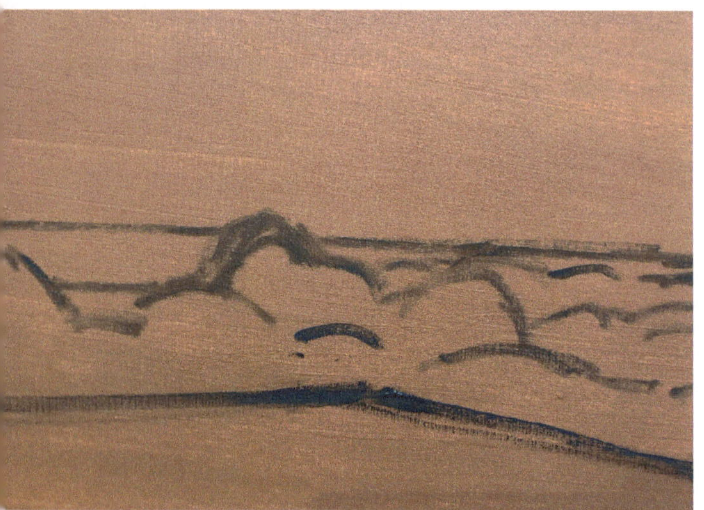

The Rule of Thirds proposes that a visual composition is most pleasing when its compositional elements conform to an imaginary set of lines that divide the frame into equal thirds, horizontally and vertically. The idea is that an off-centre composition is more satisfying and also looks more natural than one where everything is in the middle of the frame or symmetrical.

Always sketch in your composition before starting to test out how it looks. Here's an example of the one third/ two third rule exaggerated – you can do this when the land is being blended into the sky.

The two-thirds sky will extend down into the trees because of the nature of the image (see below).

The one-third line is effectively here.

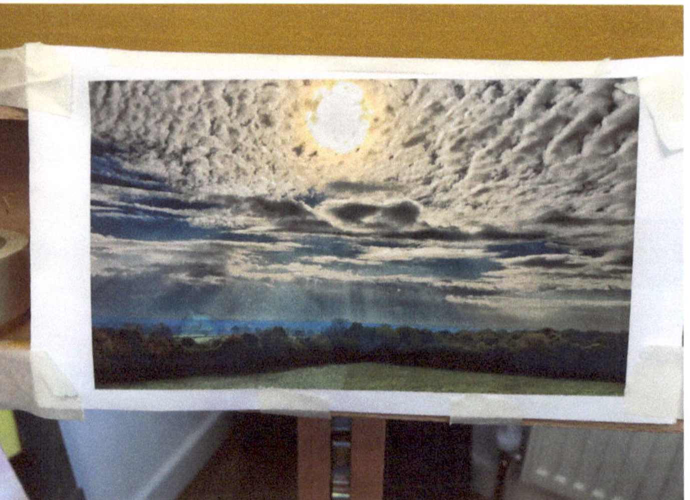

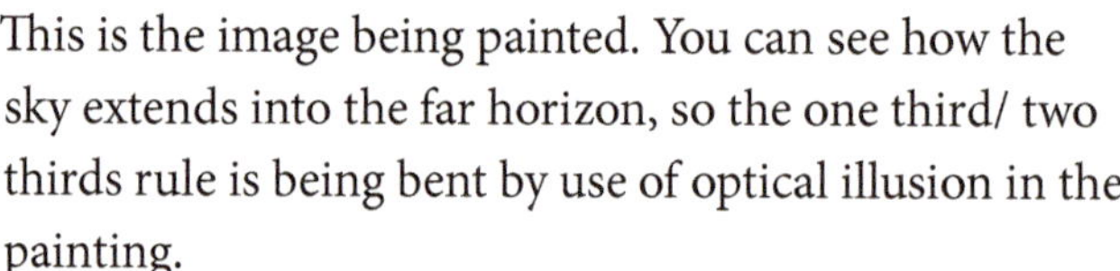

This is the image being painted. You can see how the sky extends into the far horizon, so the one third/ two thirds rule is being bent by use of optical illusion in the painting.

Special effects:

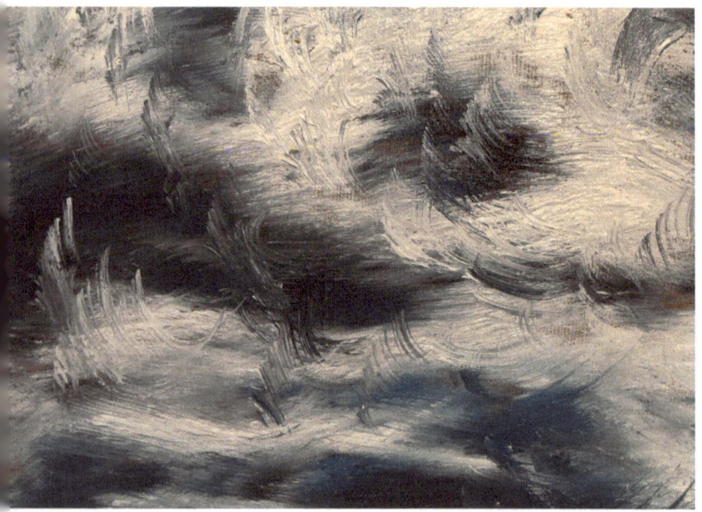

The way you paint can be as much about use of the tools you employ as colour and form. Look for the intrinsic shapes of objects and follow them with brush movements. For example, in the photograph above, the clouds are the shapes we are most concerned with; their swirling, bubbling effect. In painting them initially I mimicked this with my brush strokes, before smoothing them so the strokes morphed with the cloud movement.

You can, of course, leave brush strokes specifically obvious if they are being deliberately emphasised for a particular reason. This is called using painterly strokes. In a certain style, the brush strokes above would work best left evident. Painterly strokes can include sweeping, swirling, downward strokes, blending, partially or completely smoothing, and palette knife marks. They need to conform to your style and work with the painting itself, of course. For instance, there is a thing called the Gestalt Effect, where limited or only suggested visual information is given, leaving the brain to add the detail. It is impossible to paint in every leaf on every tree, so our shorthand version of leaves is very much Gestalt yet must still be convincing as an *impression* of leaves.

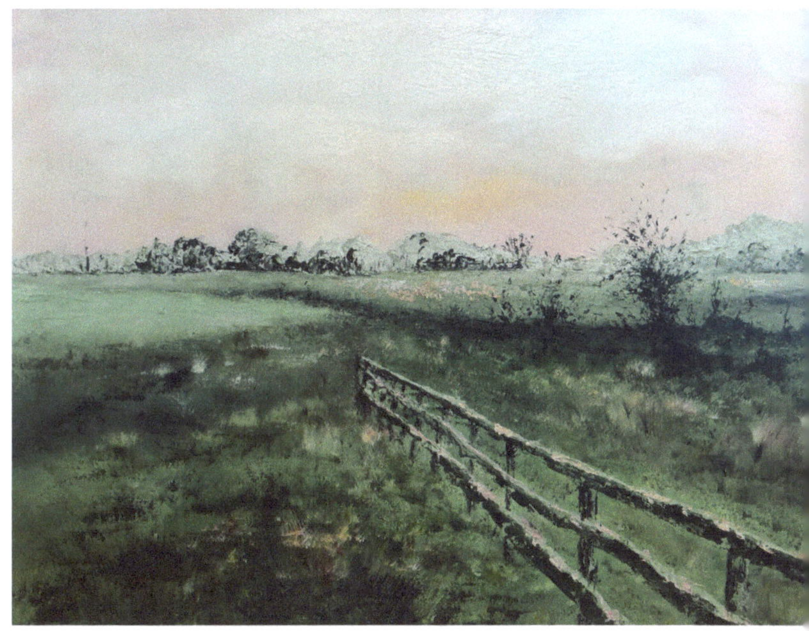

Texture is very important in painting too – whether you subscribe to smooth, sleek, old-master styles, or use layered paint to suggest form and content. Palette knives are wonderful for blocking in, Gestalt-style, or for painting impressionistically, creating branches and straight, crisp lines – but also for blurring with long sweeping strokes. This fence was painted with a palette knife in The Ridgeway, in Winter, Early Morning.

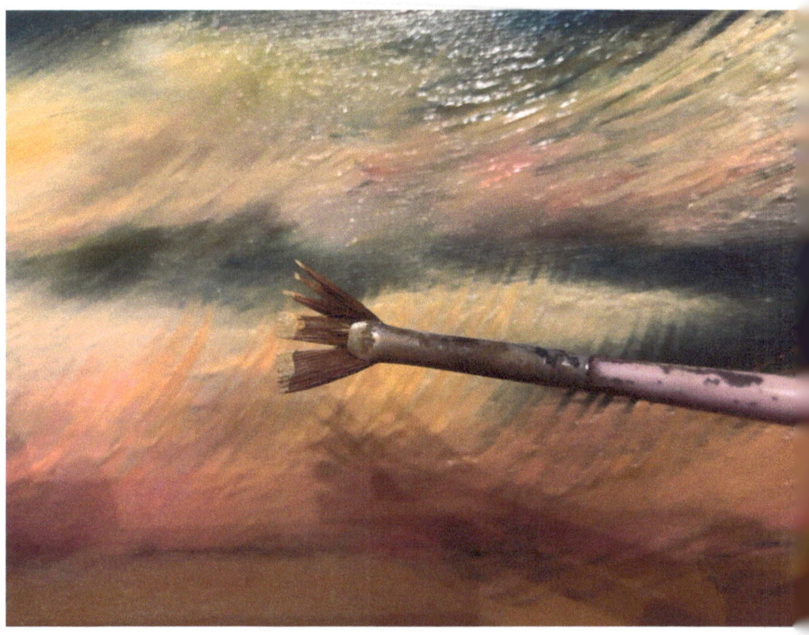

Blending is how I achieve the sfumato effect in skies. Without exception I use the three/four fan brushes I refer to in the demos throughout the book to do this.

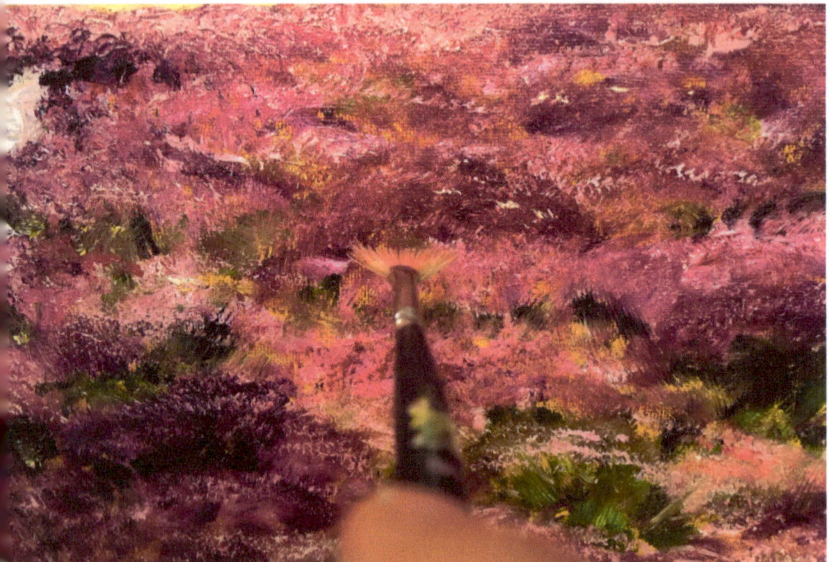

Stippling works wonderfully for foliage on trees or something like the stubbly heather in Heatherlands.

Other special effects can be obtained through the most ordinary of tools. Sponges, for example with their popped bubbles, would be perfect for creating a pebbly effect on a seashore foreground, or a crusty layer of lichen on a crumbling wall. Always look for ways to use utensils and everyday objects to creative effect – you'll be amazed and delighted with what you can do with a cotton bud or a piece of textured paper or wood … Always experiment!

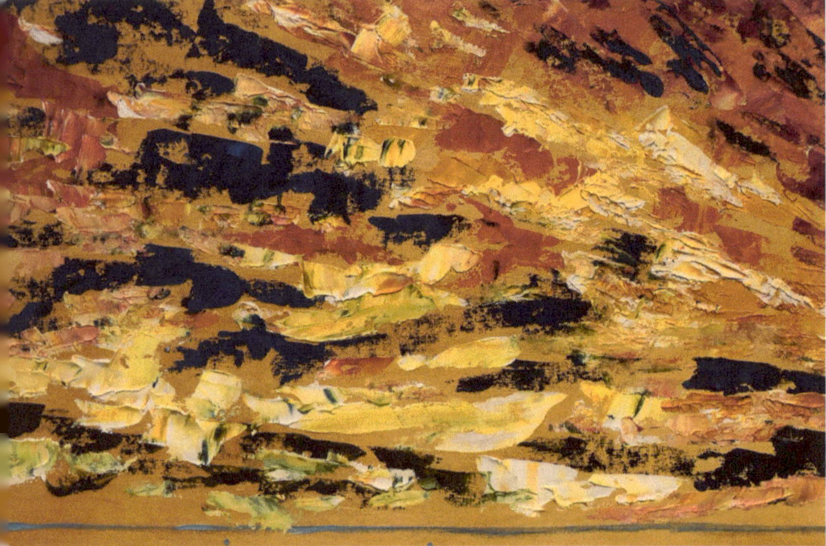

Finally, don't be afraid to be brave. Apply colour with bold sweeps and blocks of colour.

This became this – below…

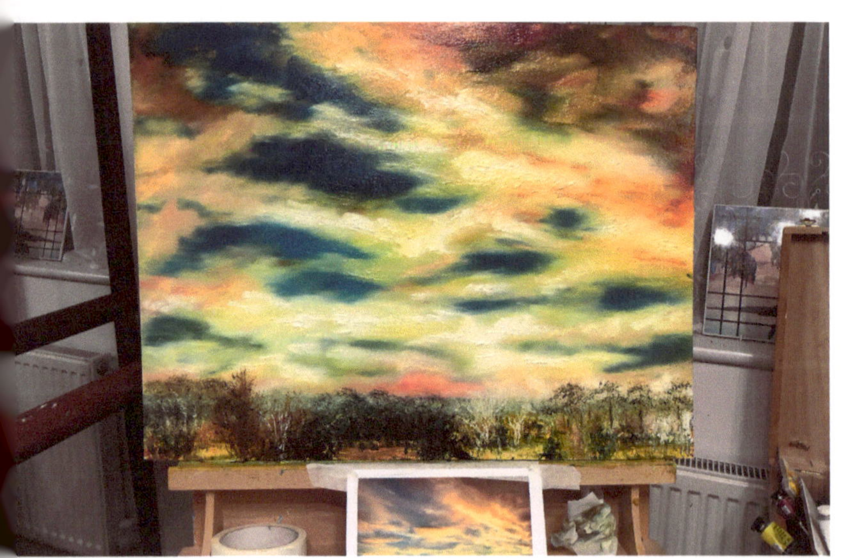

Remember how the schools of painters throughout the history of art have experimented, adapted techniques, and developed styles and different ways of seeing, so above all be prepared to see and do things differently, learning from mistakes and chalking up successes from those failures – rectified – along the way. Those blocks of colour above could equate to Seurat's pointillist paint marks, or Picasso's bold swathes. Our photographs are made up of pixels, and our perception of what we think we see, not what we really see. If you want to take a precision image, you take a photograph. If you want to create a piece of art, you paint a painting – however that might turn out. Have fun!

PART 5: THE PAINTINGS

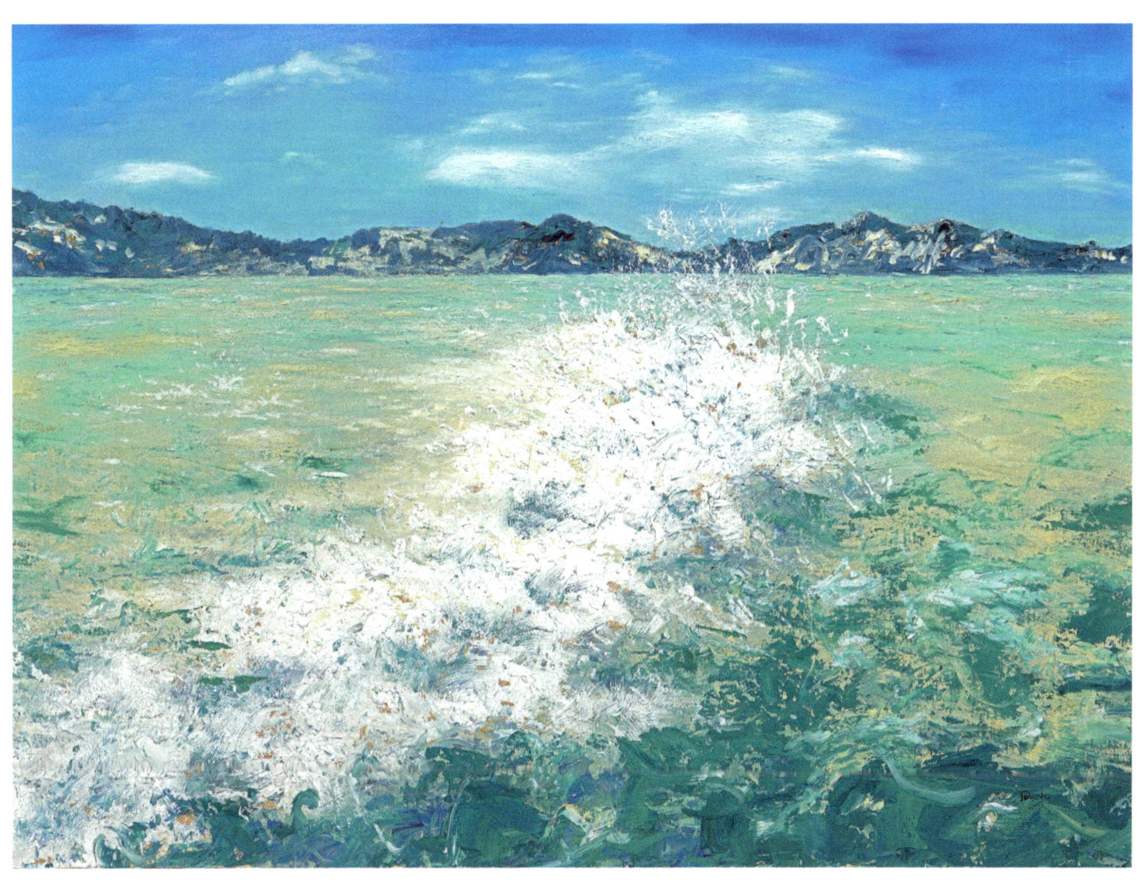

Splash

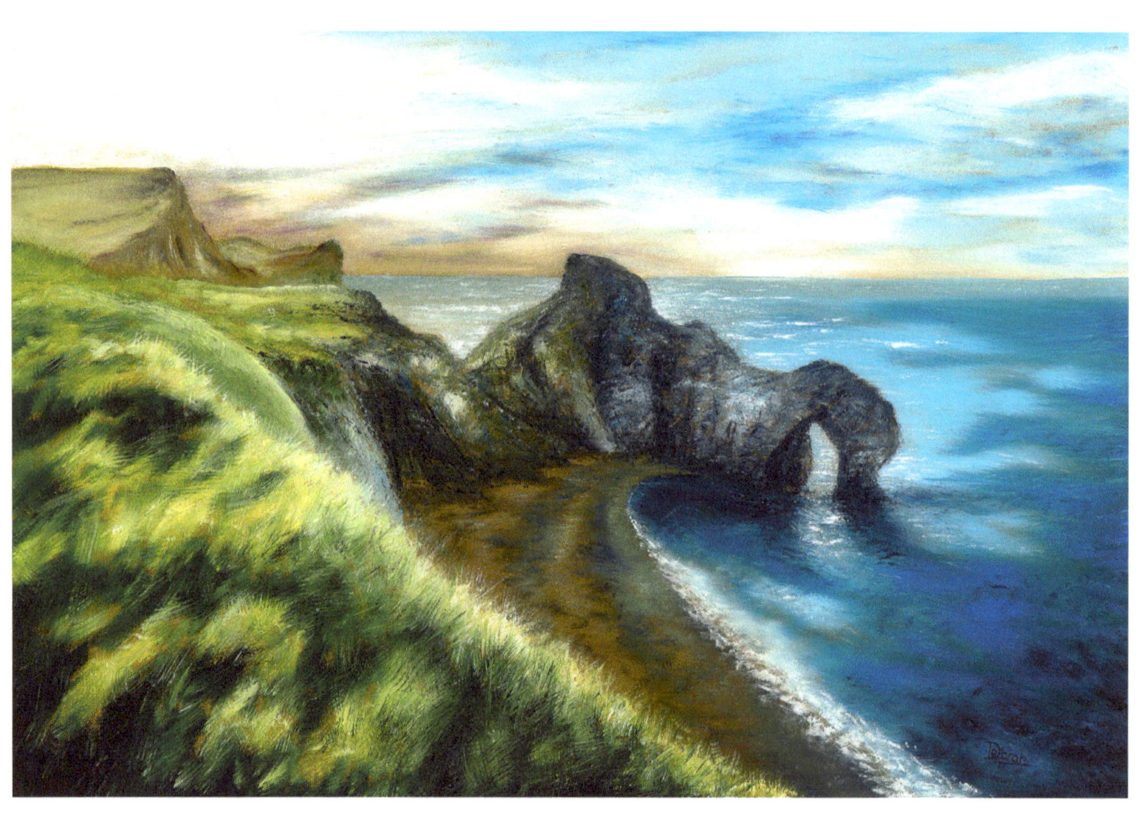

Durdle Door, Dorset

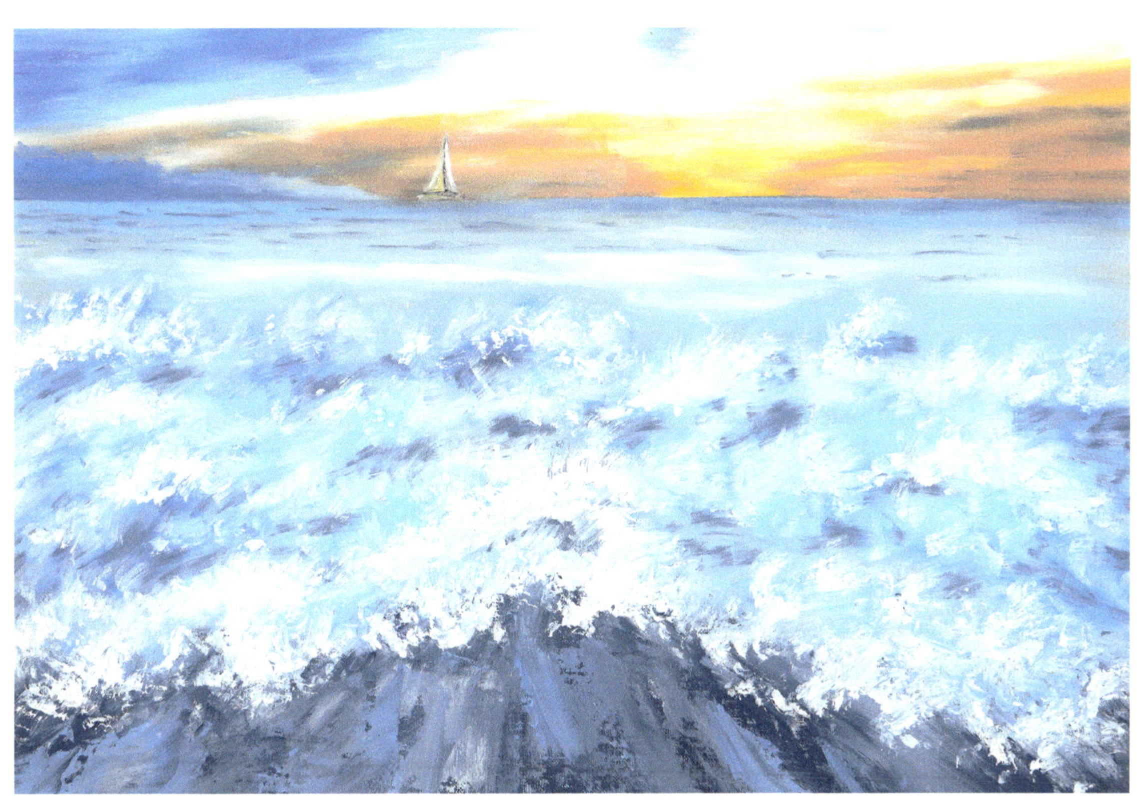

In the Distance

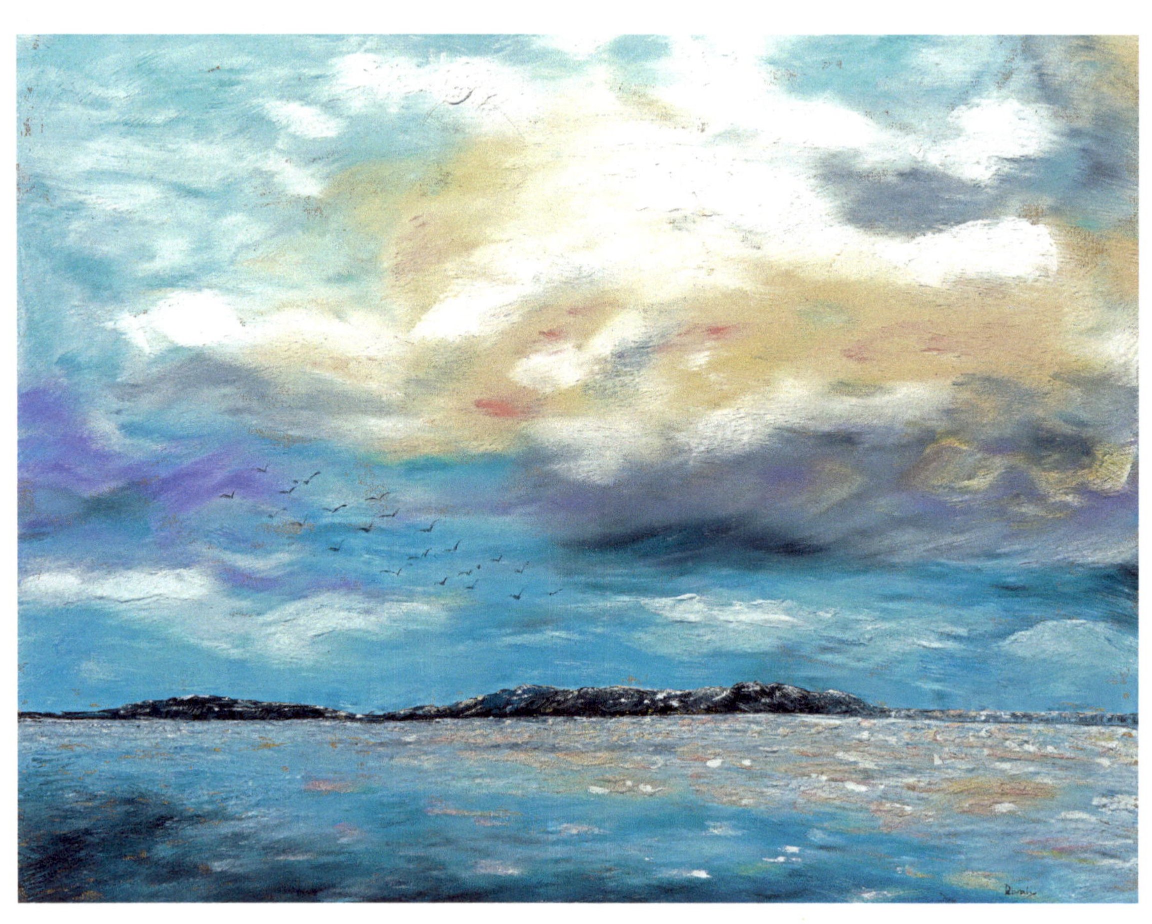

At Sea, on the Way to Akaroa, New Zealand

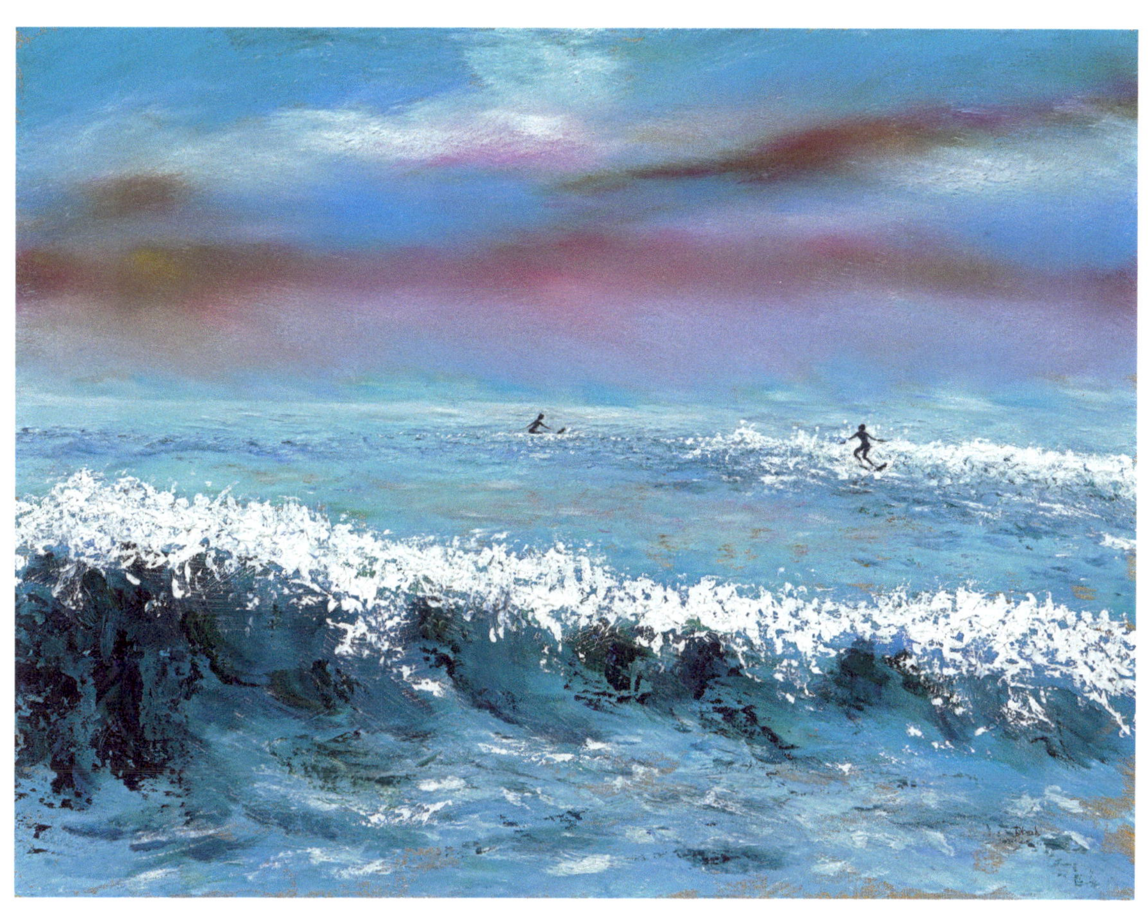

Cresting Waves, Bondi Beach

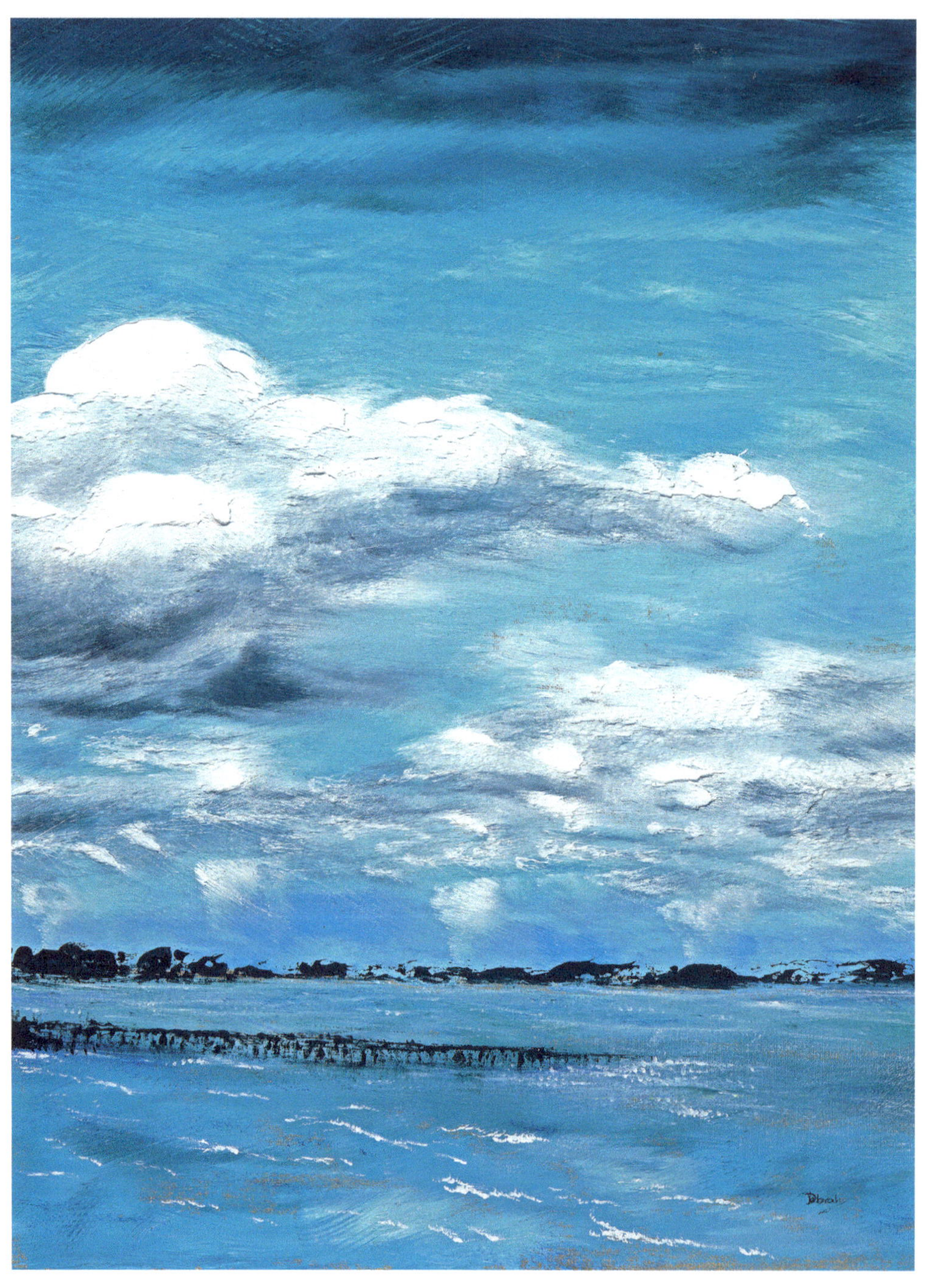

The Jetty, Dunedin, New Zealand

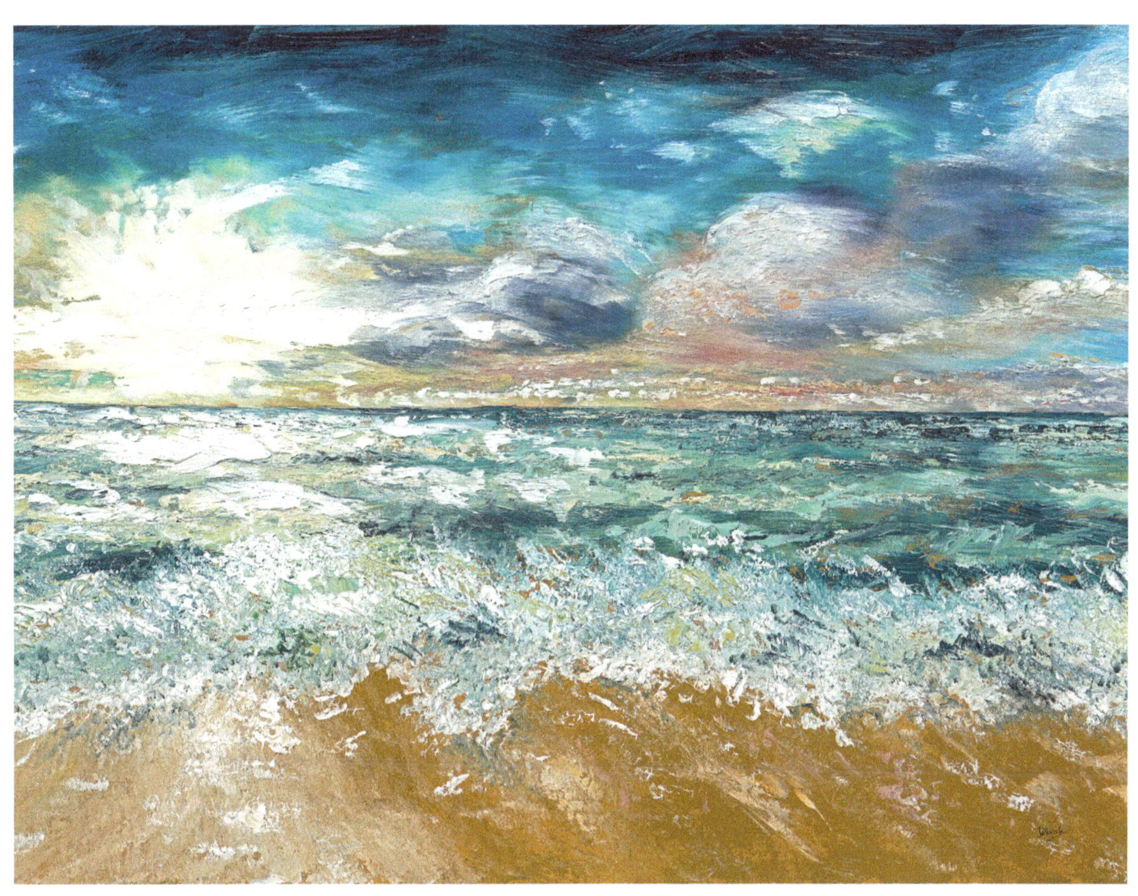

Sunset Waters

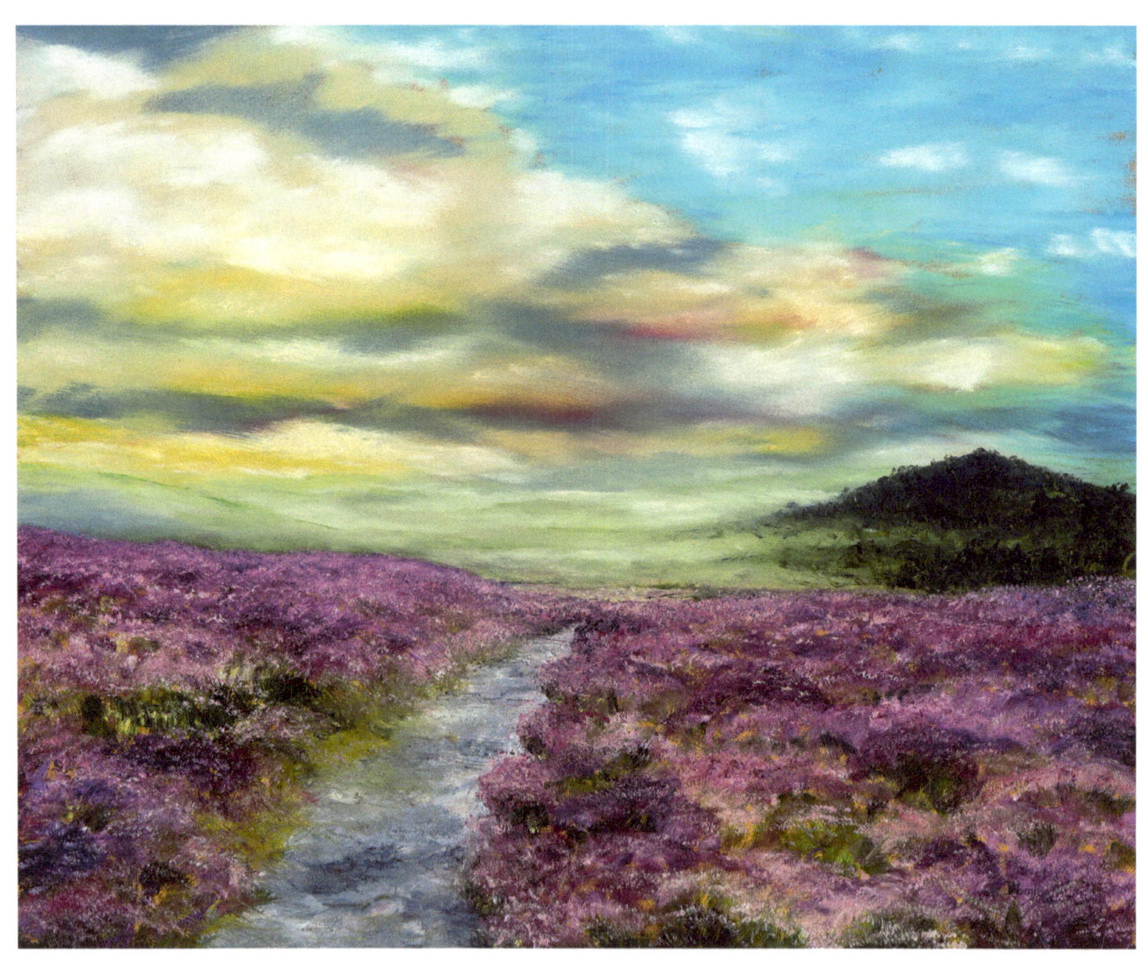

Heatherlands

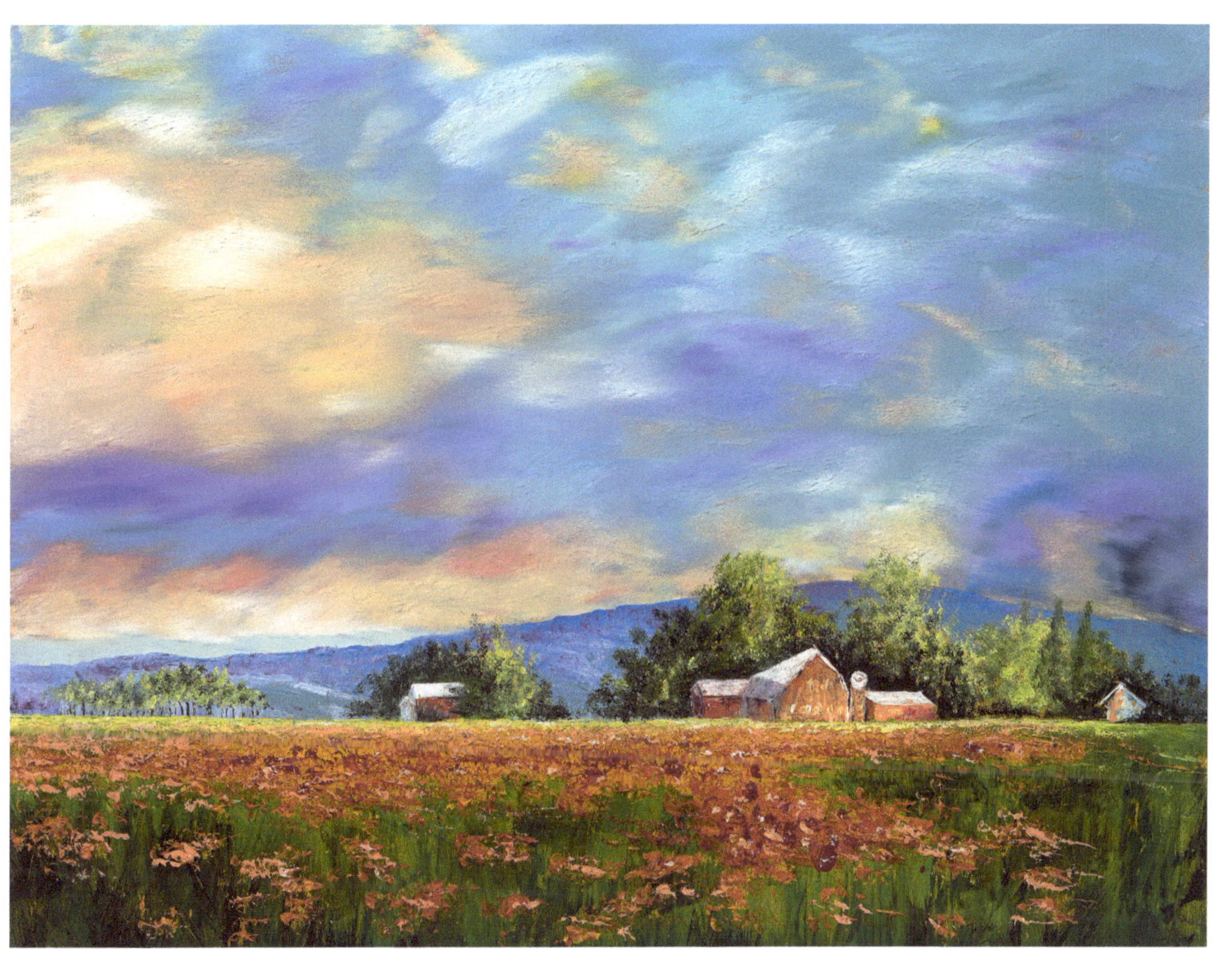

Dutch Barns and Poppies

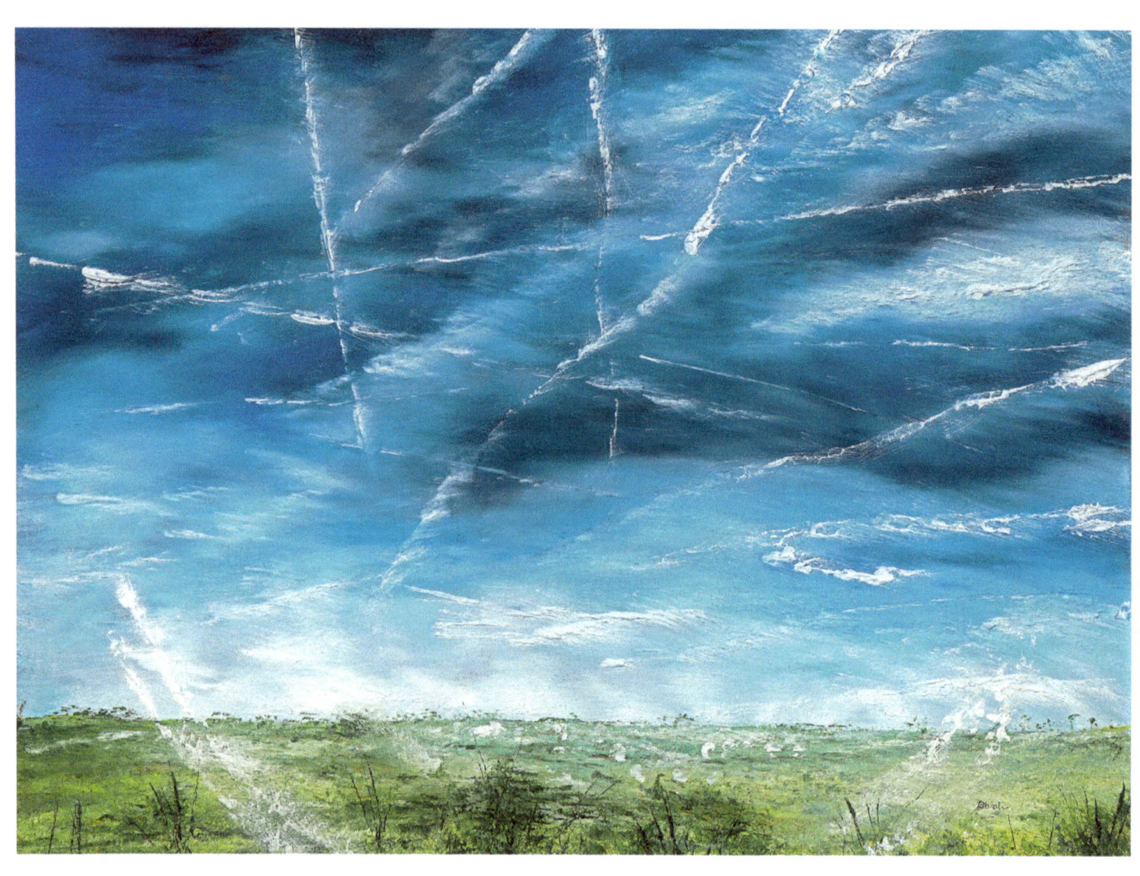

Geometric Contrails over Oxfordshire

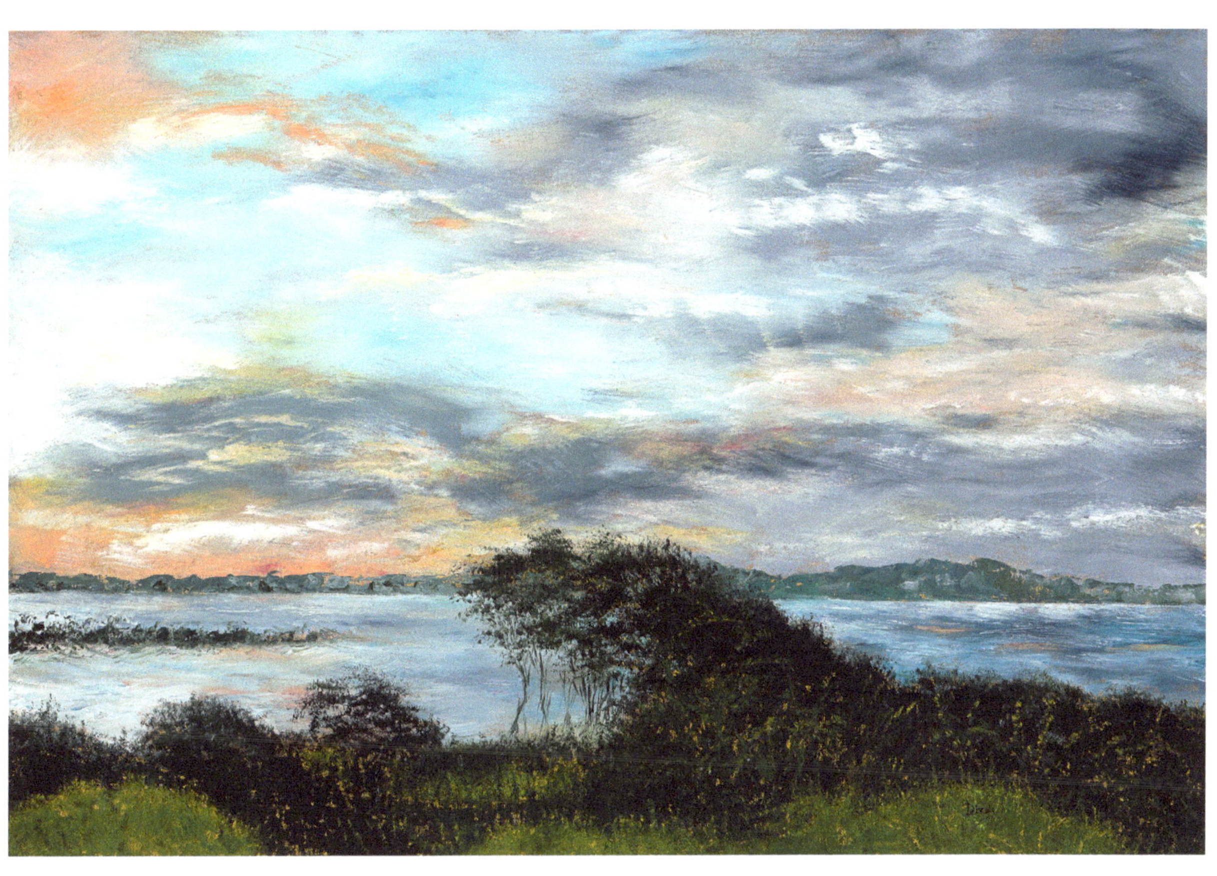

Looking out to sea from Mudbrick Vineyard, Waiheke Island, New Zealand

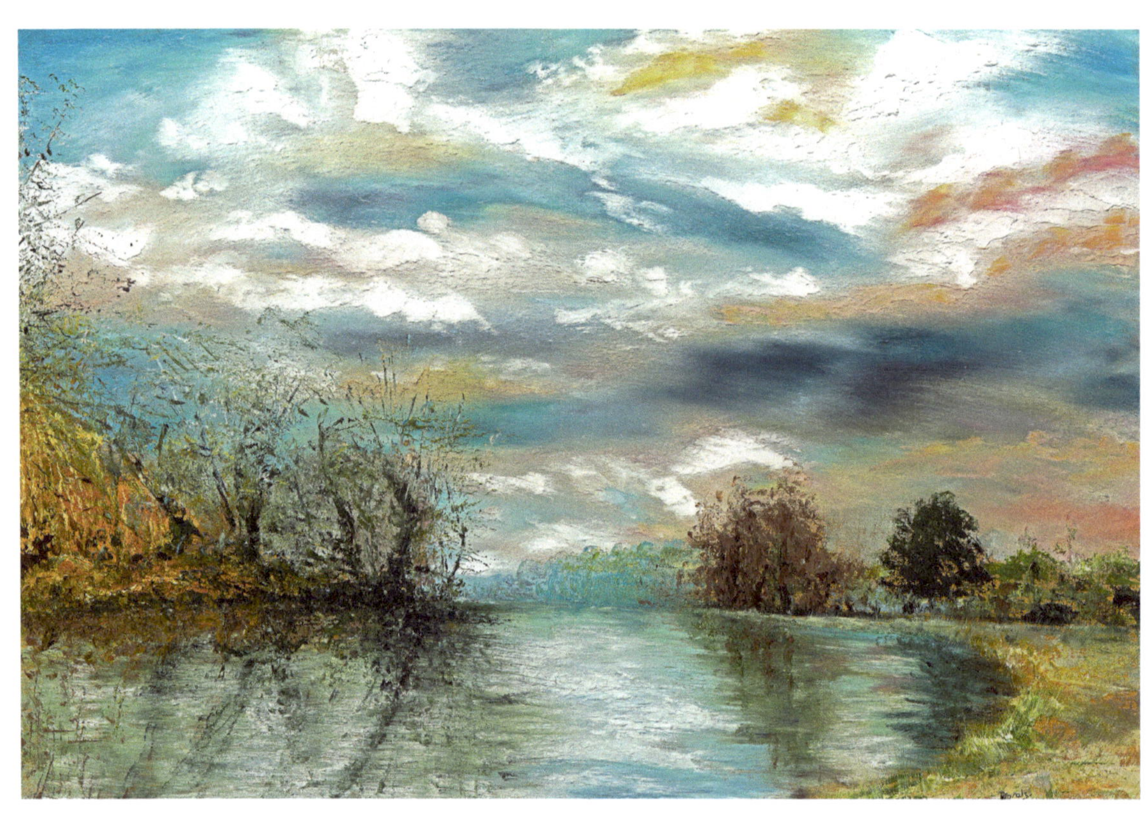

The Towpath towards Iffley Lock, Oxfordshire

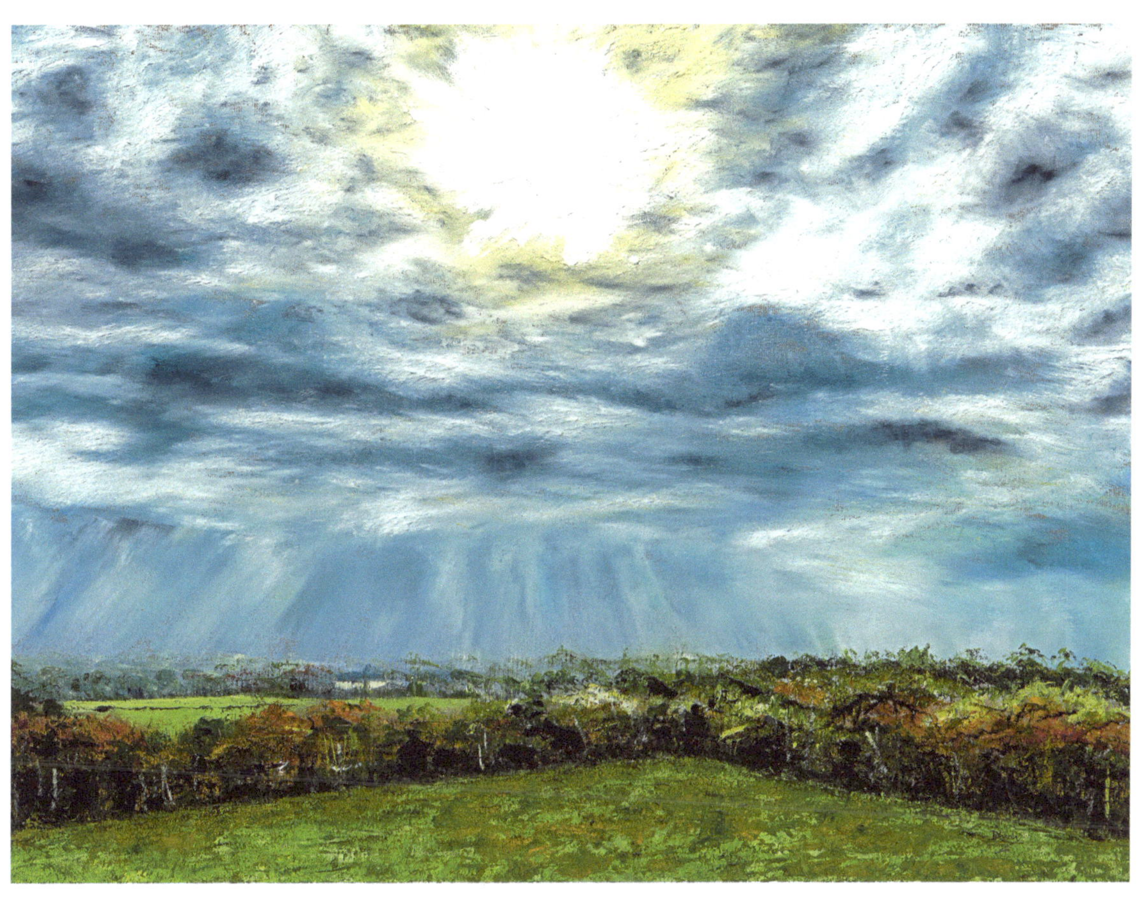

Shotover Hill, looking South; Bubbling Clouds

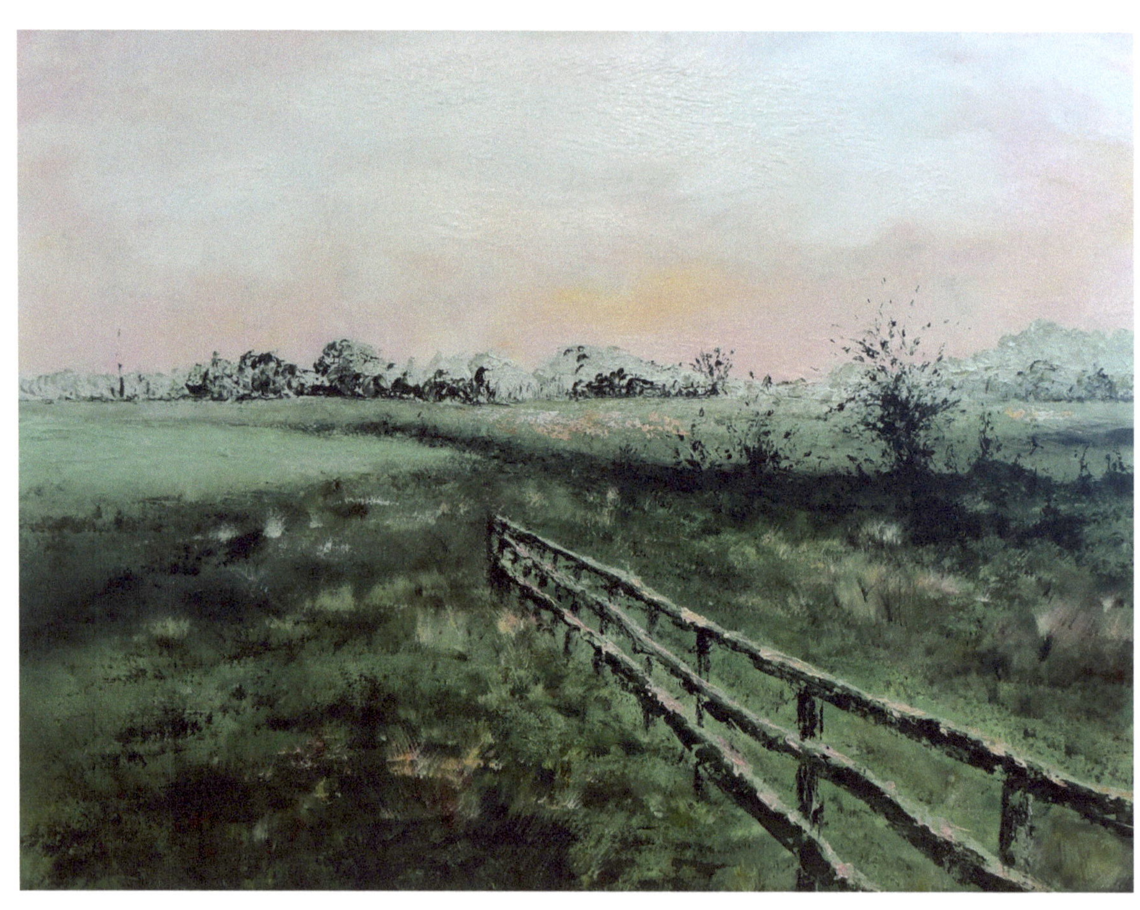

The Ridgeway, Early Morning

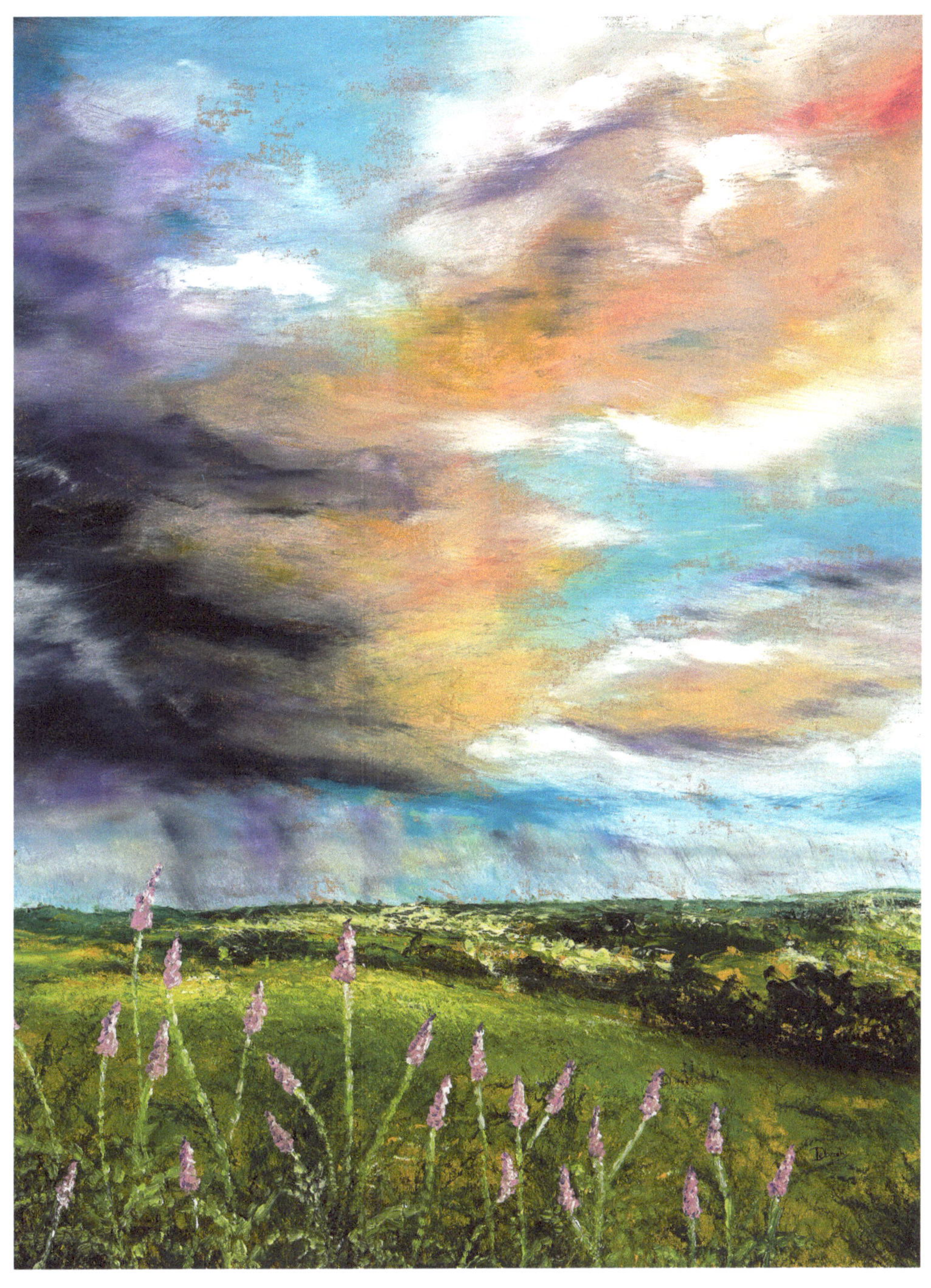

Pinks!

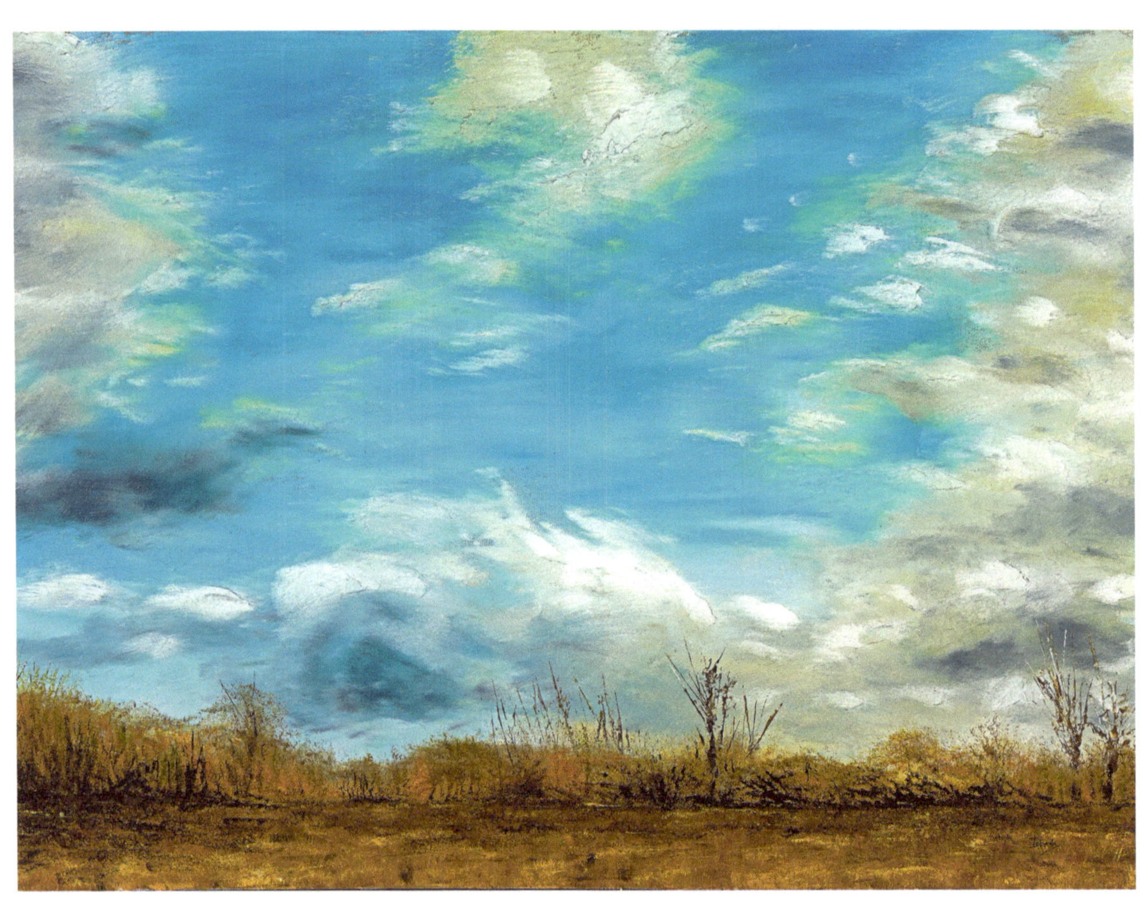

Sandford-on-Thames Clouds

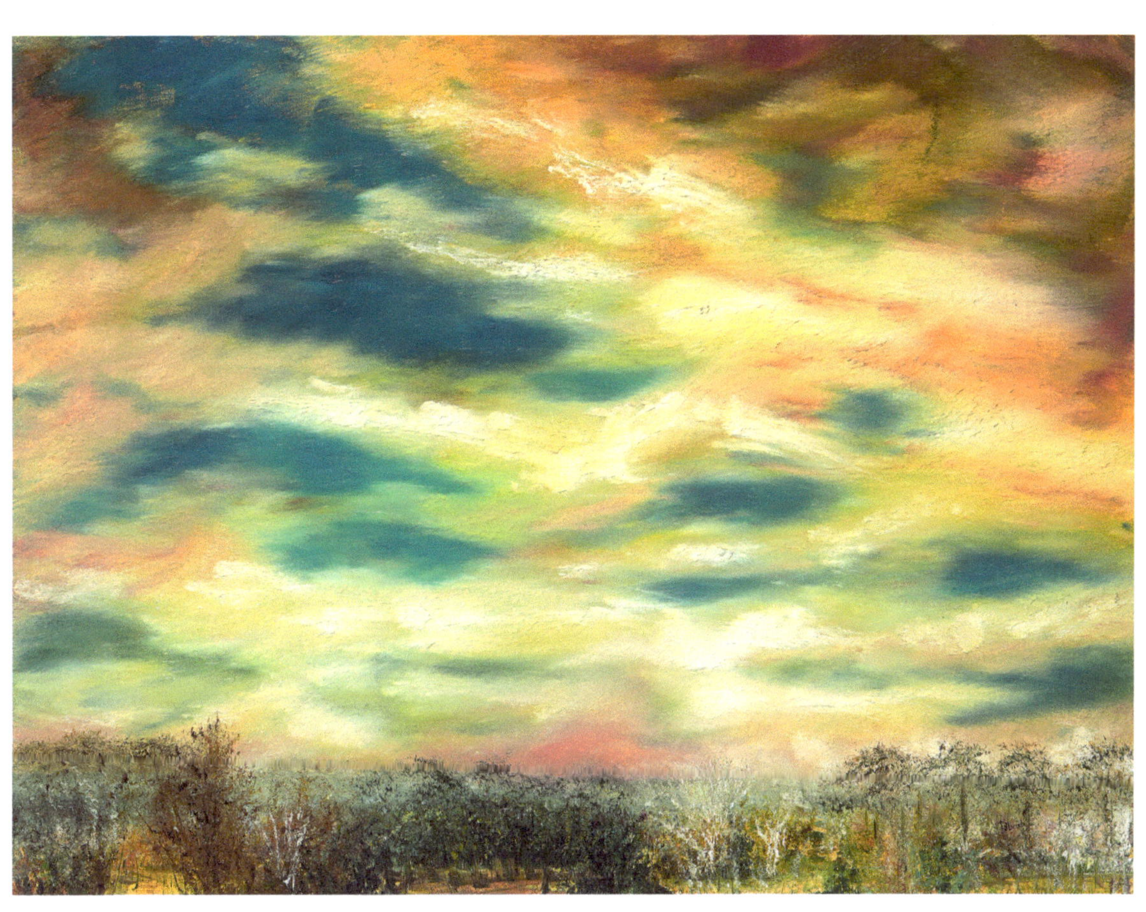

Shotover Sunset

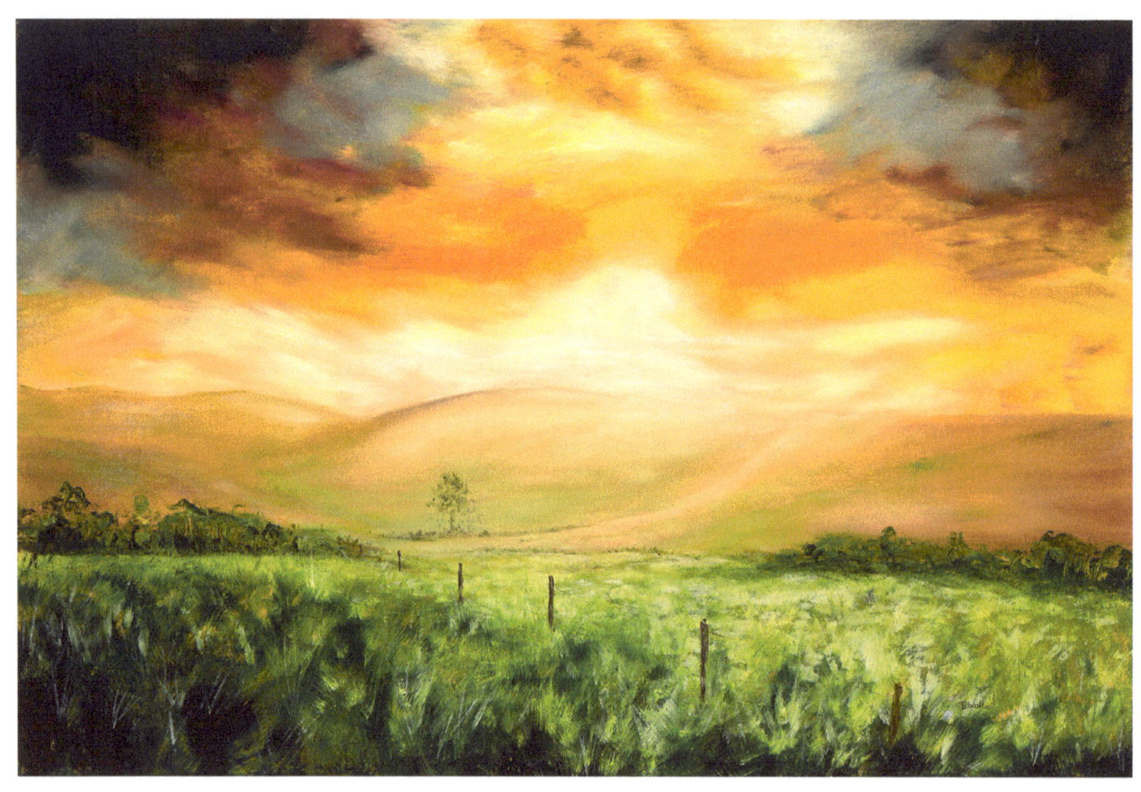

Sunset

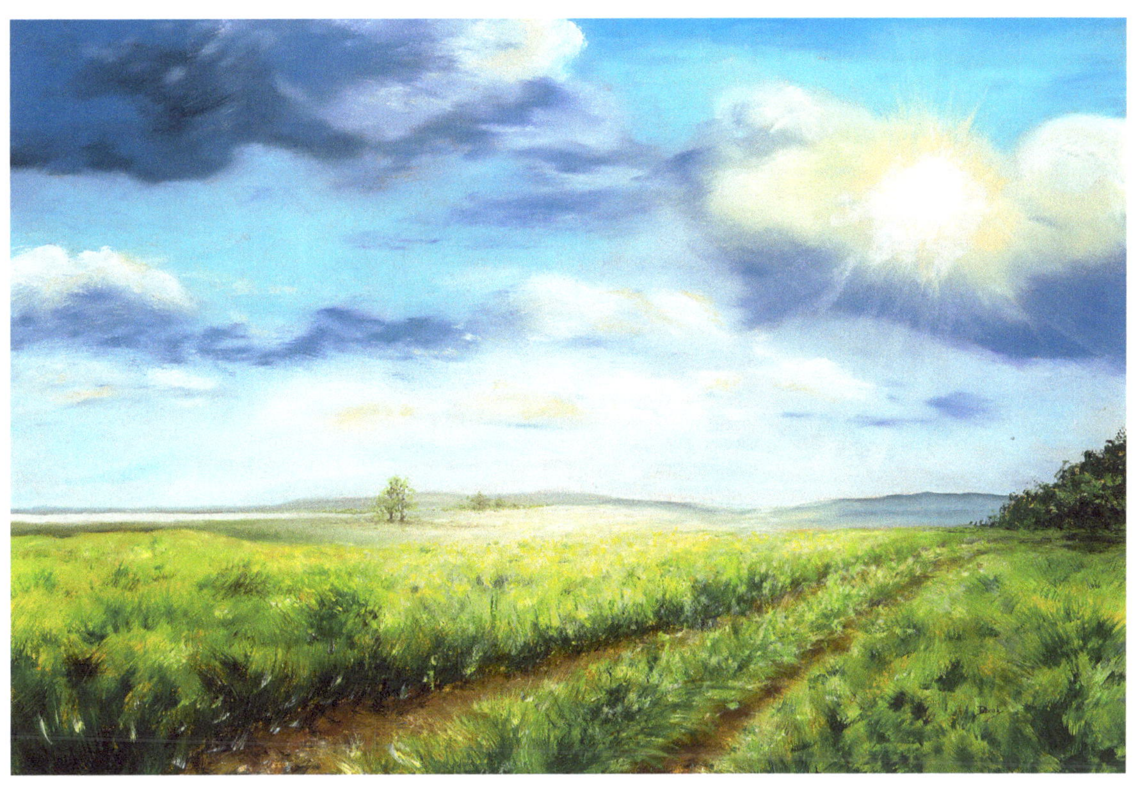

Sunlight

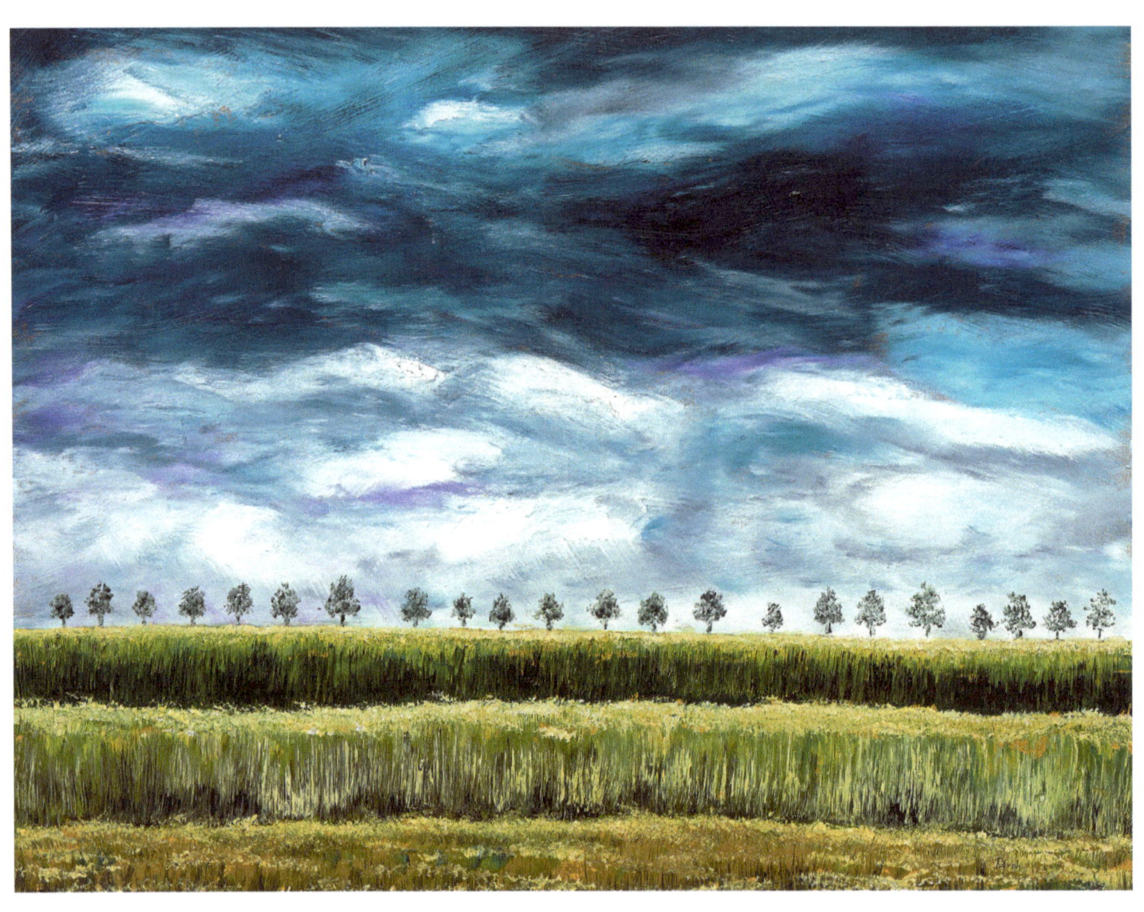

Treeline, Waiheke Island

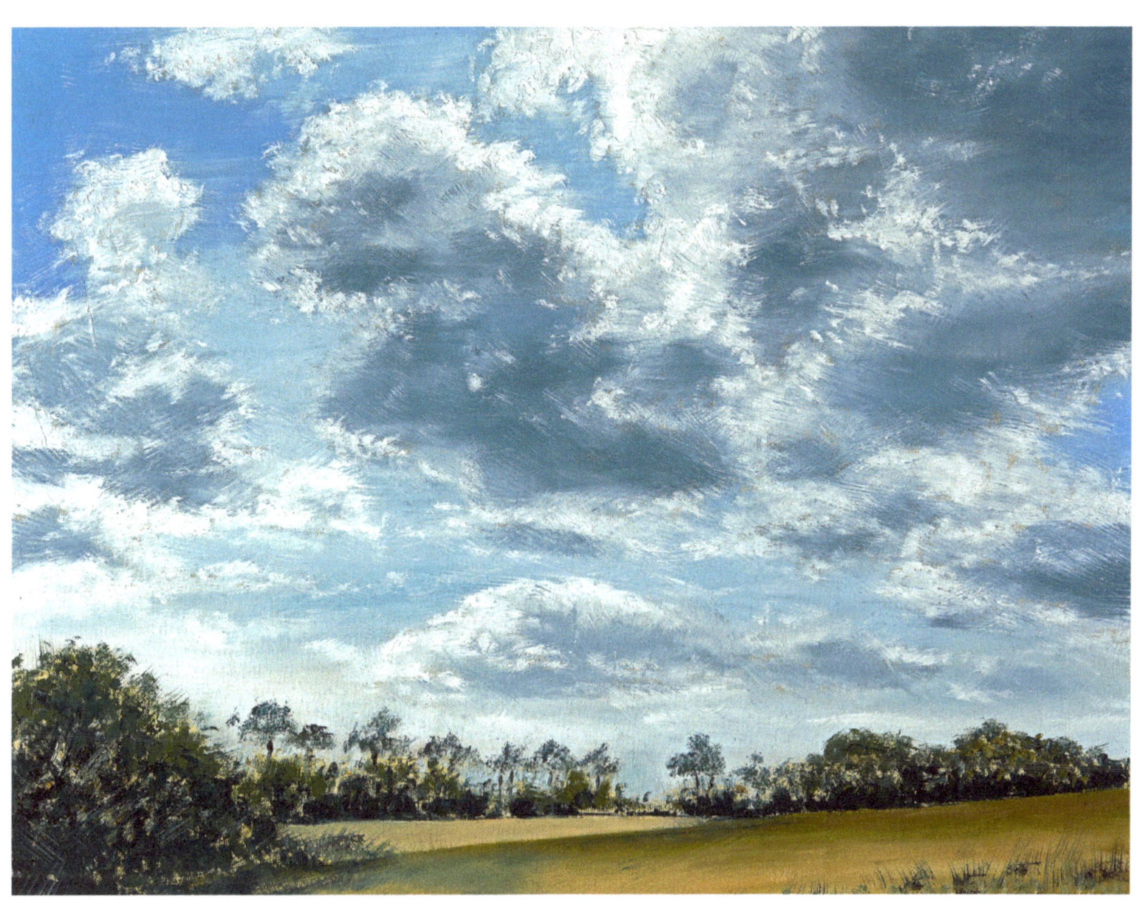

English Trees

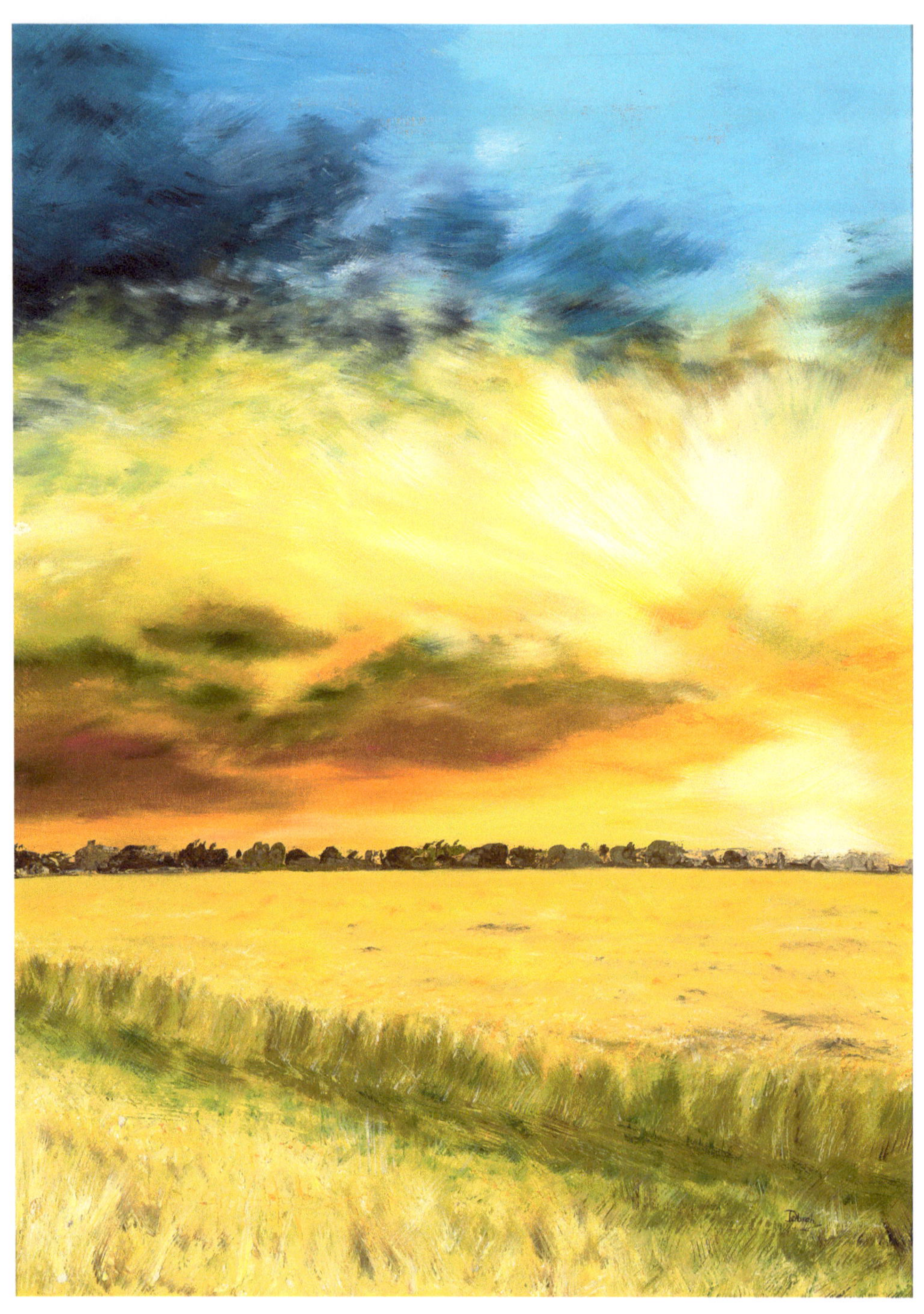

Sunset over Wheatfields

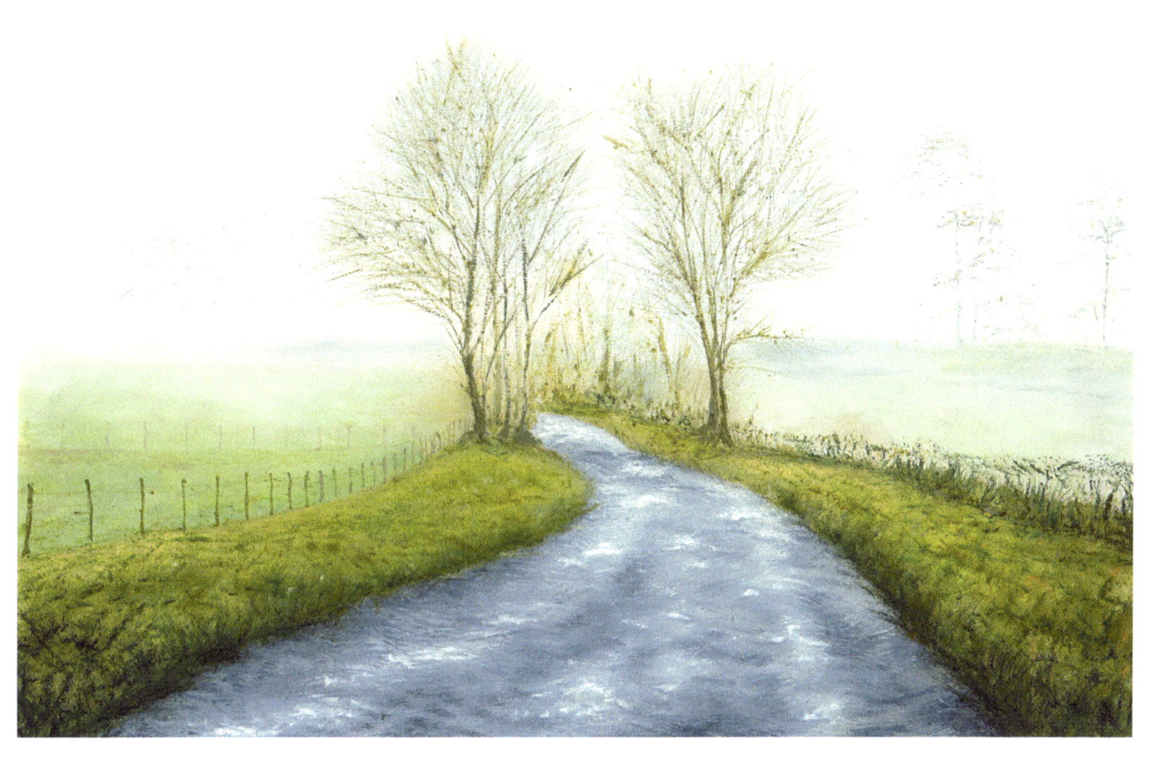

Winter is Coming

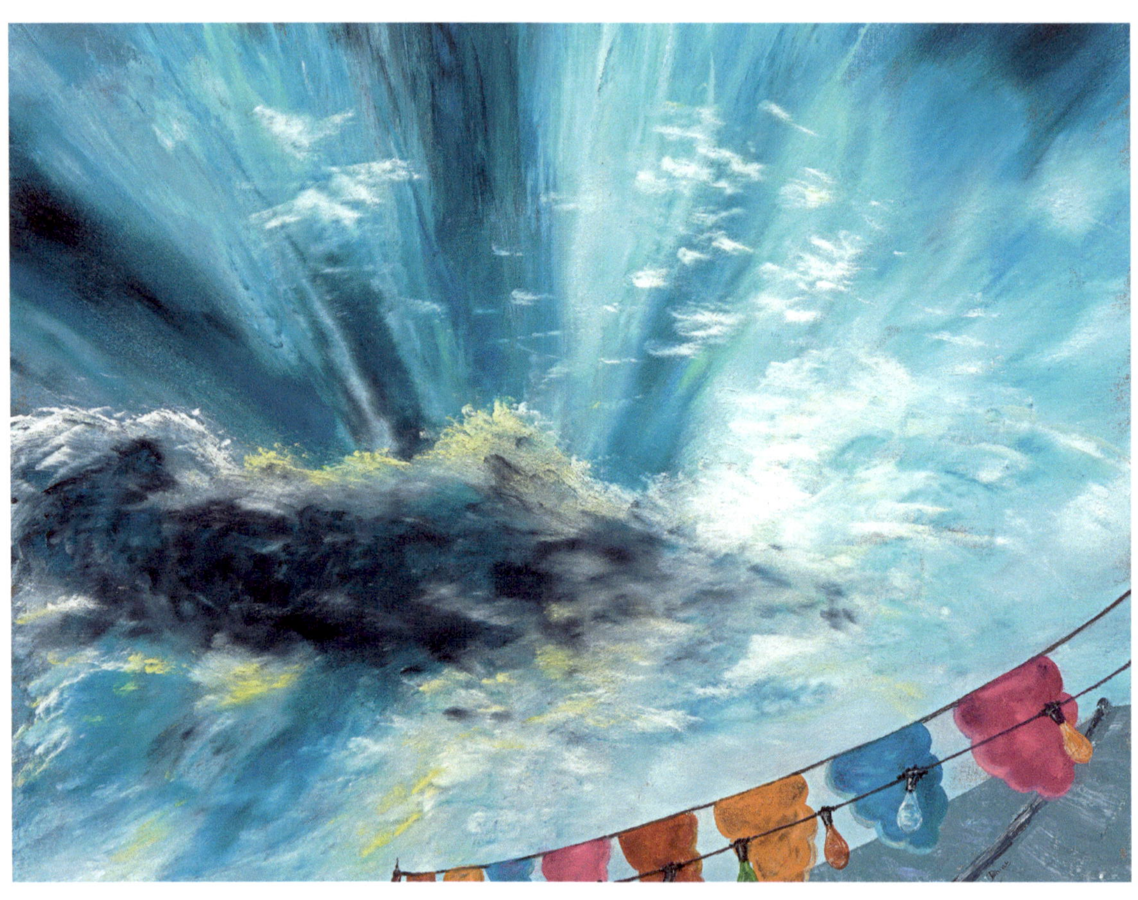

Heading for the Skies at The Common People Festival, Oxford, 2018

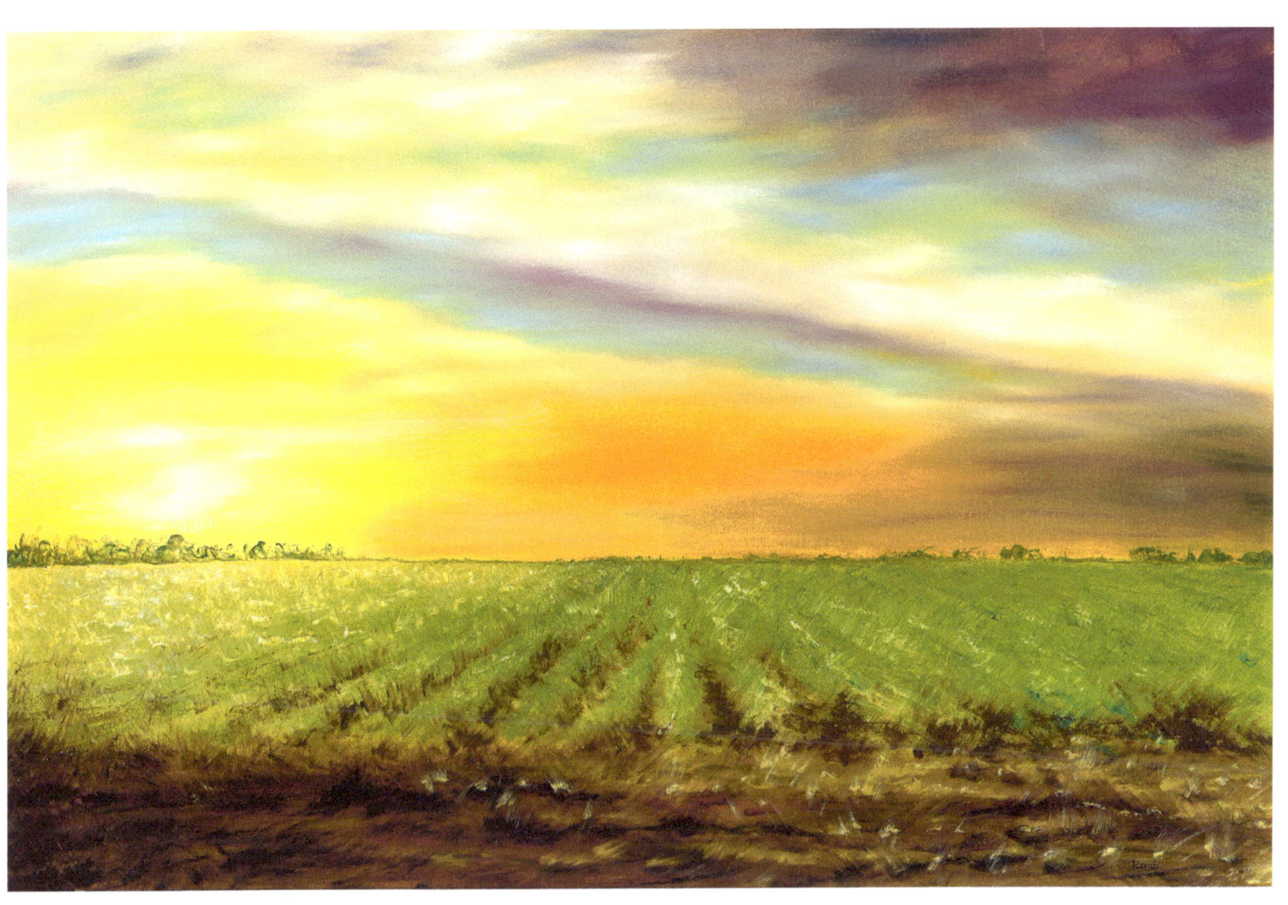

Sunrise

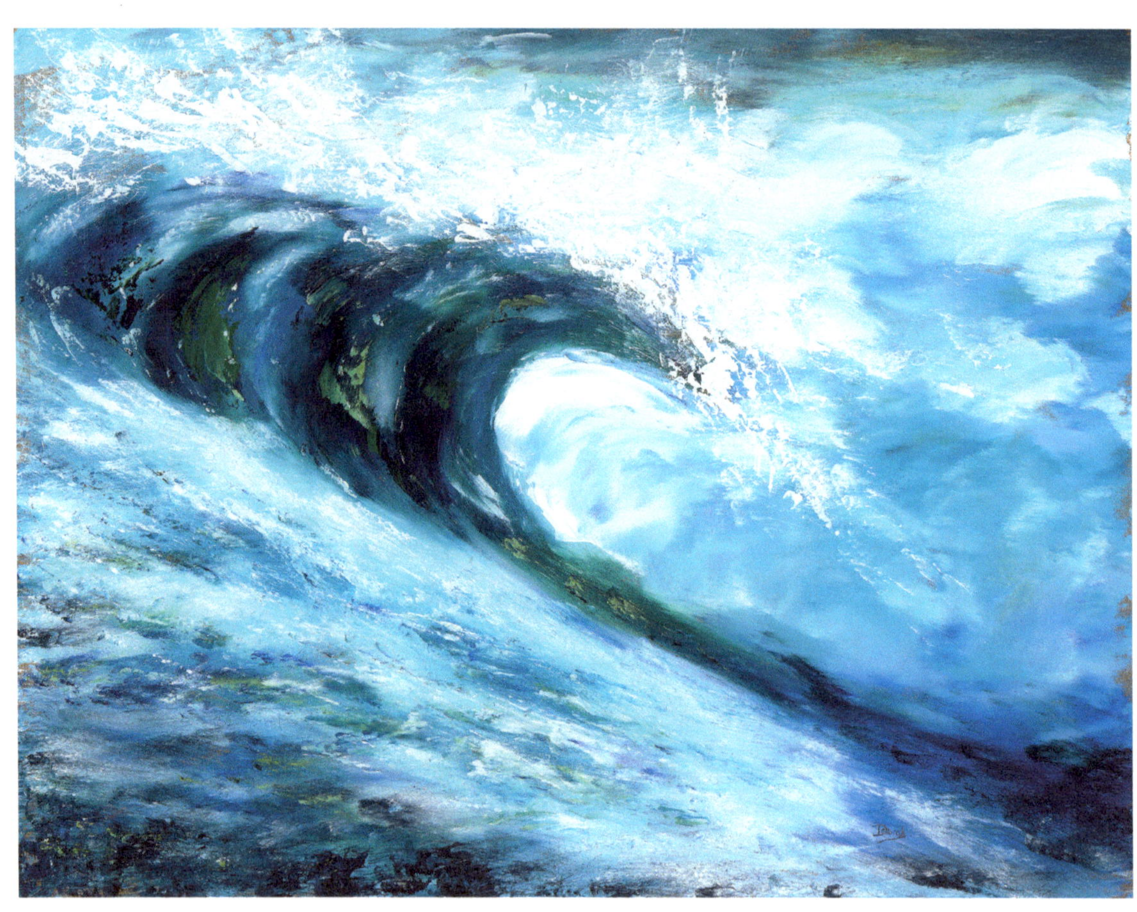

The Wave

About the Author

Debrah Martin is an artist and an author, writing psychological thriller fiction under the pen name D.B. Martin, and literary fiction under the name of Debrah Martin. Debrah also teaches, edits and mentors.

You can find out more about her books, paintings, workshops and exhibitions on her website www.debrahmartin.co.uk

Books by D. B. Martin:

Patchwork Man (Book 1 in the Patchwork People trilogy)
Patchwork People (Book 2 in the Patchwork People trilogy)
Patchwork Pieces (Book 3 in the Patchwork People trilogy)
Lady Lazarus

Books by Debrah Martin:

Falling Awake
Chained Melodies
Write, Publish, Promote
Savage Skies and Sfumato Seas